ACCUSTOMED
AS I AM

by the same author

The House About a Man
Motor If You Must
To My Embarrassment
The Whole Thing's Laughable
You Can't Be Serious
Let's Stay Married
Stay Married Abroad
Boothroyd at Bay
Philip, an informal biography
    of H.R.H. The Duke of Edinburgh (Longman)

ACCUSTOMED AS I AM

The Loneliness of the
Long-Distance Speaker
Or, All You'd Never Guess
About Public Speaking

BASIL BOOTHROYD

Illustrated by Bill Tidy

London   George Allen & Unwin Ltd
Ruskin House   Museum Street

First published in 1975

© Basil Boothroyd 1975
Illustrations © Bill Tidy 1975
ISBN 0 04 808022 5

Composition by Linocomp Ltd., Marcham, Oxon.

Printed in Great Britain by
Redwood Burn Limited
Trowbridge & Esher

Often I talk to men, of this and that,
Through the long night, and chiefly through my hat,
And they, in turn, through hats of different size,
Build confident assertion on surmise.

So it continues, hour succeeding hour,
As each small bud of thought bursts into flower,
While, listening in limbo, sit the sages,
The Great Ones of the contemplative ages,
And all the sons of knowledgeable Man
Who ever talked since Time itself began —
Listening now, eager to catch one glow
Of thought not born five thousand years ago,
One little curtain raised, one tiny pelmet,
One word not said through some old Roman helmet.

Philip Stalker

(By kind permission of the proprietors of *Punch*)

Contents

Speaker's Foreword

This isn't about public speaking. It's about me public speaking. If the vertical pronoun sticks up all over it like an establishing shot of Manhattan Island, it's disgraceful but can't be helped. Few other activities demand the towering ego on this scale. It may only have to tower for five minutes (toast to the happy couple), twenty (response for the guests), forty (study group of British Weatherwear Stockists), or sixty (practically all ladies' Literary Circles, who are as keen as the next lady on getting their money's worth). But tower it must. Before and after you can be yourself, a frightened girl. But while you're up and going, let no dog bark.

I don't know anything about other speakers' methods. Mine are complicated and inefficient, cluttered with enough psychological blocks to make Father Freud leave the business, so if you pick up a tip or two it'll only be incidental. You may learn, perhaps, not to turn up at Tonbridge when it ought to be Tunbridge Wells, to steer clear of the standing audience, to have no qualms about the removal of platform flowers which, as sited, would only leave your ears showing; not to make jokes about electricity at electricity conventions, or gas at gas conventions, though the opposite goes well at either, nor, on a civic occasion, to ask a neighbour, 'Who's the little fat man with the brass chain?' before checking if the microphone's live.

But none of this is the point. I'm just stating the case for the man on his feet. There he stands, confidently beaming, band-box fresh, dominant as a tree on a plain. What do they know, who put him there, of his vain regrets and bloody sweats? Or his conviction that the free-standing buttonhole flap on his evening shirt, having no matching button on these particular trousers, has escaped its safety-pin and juts forth like a tiny handshake?

He enters their life for an hour, filling a speaker-shaped space like a fairground cut-out. How should they guess that it's not an hour, but a week, out of his life, mostly with bad nights and delirious mutterings? Why, when he's gone, should they give him another thought, as he lurks at a cabless Euston, or sprints for the Cincinnati plane?

I knew a guileless playwright who was asked to lecture on The Theatre, in a Sussex village. He was new to the thing, but conscientious, and researched in depth to get together sixty minutes' good stuff, all the way from Aristophanes to Tom Stoppard, with sub-plots on the unities, Stanislavsky, Shaw's prefaces and the Baconian theory.

'Ah,' said the lady of the manor, greeting him at the Memorial Hall by his wrong name, a thing that we old sweats take in our stride. 'Do you play the piano?' He did. Could he oblige with three verses of 'The Church's One Foundation'? He could. The ladies of the Wednesday Afternoon Culture Club struggled up and sang the club anthem:

> 'We are the happy circle,
> The girls of Walton Green,
> We gather every Wednesday,
> No fairer sight is seen . . .'

As he played he revised, redrafted, jettisoned. No one had told him that his audience would be elderly, female and, if he wasn't misjudging them on short acquaintance, strangers to Aristophanes and perhaps even to Agatha Christie.

He launched off eventually. A minute into his script, a

door opened from some obscure side-chapel and a girl in faintly clinical costume called ringingly, 'Mrs Acland!' A member of the audience was helped up and out, soon to return to summon Mrs Armstrong, who came back pageing Miss Bates. He estimated that they got about twenty-five of them in and out before he'd finished, all the exits and entrances coming on his best lines.

'Splendid,' said the devil-woman who'd landed him with all this. 'Did you enjoy it?' The question is often asked, enshrining misconceptions, and he made the only possible answer. Very much indeed. But – affecting polite interest – what exactly had been going on? 'I'm so glad you asked,' she said, 'because this is entirely *my* idea. When they have their little talks on alternate Wednesdays, the man comes from Brighton and does their feet.'

Between the speaker and the spoken to there is a great gulf fixed. I always think of the incident as a good, if limited, example.

Chapter 1

A Little Throat-Clearing

I nearly wrote this book ten years ago. So nearly that it appeared in *Who's Who* until 1972. And then disappeared, a mystery that makes the Marie Celeste seem an open and shut case.

Everyone, the myth goes, has an unwritten book in him. How many have unwritten a book? What happened? There must be some perfectly simple explanation, as they keep saying in the radio plays, and if you aren't on the edge of your seats, ladies and gentlemen, eager to know it, I've misjudged this whole speech so far and had better switch to the story of Mary Pickford and the Indonesian photographer.

I never wrote it, is the answer. I meant to. I wanted to. I was so sure I should that I claimed it when the next edition's proofs came round. But it never got written, and I was too weak to take it out again. Reduce that scanty stock of published titles? I couldn't bring myself. If I'd had the sense to say it was 'in preparation', it would have made an honest man of me. A useful device for those who mean to write something or other one of these days, once they can get the garden under control. 'In preparation, A Technical

Study of the Aluminium Easy-Open Ring-Pull Beer-Can.'
Or the lives of all the Popes.

Thank you. I believe the gentleman at the back has a question. If I didn't take it out, who did? All in good time, my dear sir.

It's an indispensable volume, *Who's Who*, for chairmen of dinners, presidents of arts guilds, Lord Mayors' Remembrancers, and all who realise that their guest speaker is someone they've never heard of, and they'd better get a quick rundown before introducing him by saying that he needs no introduction.

So for ten years, as I smirked idiotically through these preliminaries, the gastric juices working overtime to disperse the water-ice stuck under my wish-bone, I was always amused, or as near as an imminent speech permits, to hear them pick out the unwritten book for special mention and even praise. 'Though I have not, myself, been fortunate enough to read . . .'

But the day came when a chairman annoyed me. It may have been the man who introduced me as Mr Ernest Dudley, the Armchair Detective, for whom I was deputising at short notice. Either no one had told him or he didn't care, because he introduced me with Mr Dudley's introduction. But no. The chap I'm thinking of trotted out my unwritten work, which he wouldn't have looked up if he'd got the wrong guest.

Was it at one of those young politicians' evenings? It sounds possible. They're pretty breezy affairs, where the twenty members of the audience are having such a great, screaming time when you turn up that it seems a shame to start the business of the evening and spoil the fun. It doesn't, in fact, start for some time, even when the meeting has been called to order with cries of 'Good old Fred!' and some spirited banter over who's going to get landed with the three-legged chair this time.

There's usually a lot of preliminary business to be got through: the treasurer's well-heckled appeal for overdue subscriptions; a vote on the summer outing; the reading of amusing postcards from members on holiday; and the minutes of the last meeting, with emphasis on the excellence of the speaker they had that time.

But no, again. I'd hardly have turned on those young politicos. So high-spirited. So mysteriously non-political. So understandably complacent, having found that even meeting every fortnight they can always find someone to come and air his ego for the price of a coffee and biscuit.

Perhaps it was that grand dinner and ball in Blackpool, the chairman brave in a blue enamel necklace. It was partly my fault for not checking the arrangements. This is always advisable. There's nothing worse than turning up to auction a cake, and finding you're down for a thirty-minute speech. Unless it's turning up with a thirty-minute speech and finding you're only down to auction a cake.

My mistake this time was in thinking there wouldn't be any other speeches, apart from the conventional topping and tailing. So when I saw from the menu that I should be following eight toasts, honouring every aspect of the organisation's activities from chess club to Old Folks Coal Fund, with lots of in-jokes and those sudden bursts of applause that strand the outsider between two sorts of smile, the uncomprehending bonhomous and the bogus appreciative, I spent the time dismantling my material and reassembling it in shorter and shorter forms. I even toyed with the idea of abandoning it altogether, and basing an impromptu substitute on chess, old folks, and other more immediate material.

But I'd once been caught like that, in a mood of over-confidence at the Colchester Oyster Feast, where I was to follow comedian Jimmy Edwards. Following comedians is never good. This time it was bad. He'd also decided to go impromptu, and the speech I'd planned to hang mine on took the form of a longish recital on a euphonium handed down from the musicians' gallery. A hard lesson, but worth learning.

As to Blackpool, I'd also had a bad experience in the train. Time was going to be short at the other end. Being

alone in the compartment, I decided to change on the way, and achieved this, except for the dinner jacket, before going along to take tea in the nearby restaurant car. Tea in full regalia seemed excessive. I covered my frills with a sweater, and closed cheerfully with the fish-paste sandwiches.

Heading back to the compartment past one of those grille-sided guard's vans I found my way barred by a locked door, and asked the guard if he could unlock it. 'A could,' he said (a local man), but tha'd be out on't track.' It seemed that my part of the train had been slipped during tea, but if I got out at the next station and waited an hour it would, in some mysterious way I've never understood, which, as the guard explained it, sounded like the Binomial Theorem with loop lines, come round again.

It was distressing to find that the next station was Wigan. It isn't Wigan's fault that it's a joke in its own right, but you can't blink the facts. We humorists, waiting on any station in half evening dress for a train to draw in with our scattered lingerie and hairbrushes, already feel that life's serious side has turned on us. At Wigan it's worse, because the story can never be told. The Wigan part falsifies it into music-hall invention, and feeble at that. There's a way out,

I suppose. Change it to Hatfield, or some other location free of the built-in titter, and it might work. But it would mean some timetable research for the incidental details. There's bound to be a man in the audience who favours the ABC for bedtime reading, and he'll be down on you at question-time like George Bradshaw in person.

All this meant a late arrival at the Imperial, Blackpool – which, come to think of it, may have been the Grand, Eastbourne, and if so will prompt a sharp challenge from ABC men on how Hatfield got in. The danger with spending your life telling stories about the way it treats you is that you can keep improving the material and losing the facts.

For me, an essential speech preliminary is an hour alone in a quiet room, with bath, stretch-out, and any radio programme that has nothing to do with the spoken word. Recordings of *Judas Maccabaeus* are good, if you can find them. This is difficult in America, where the hotel-room radio has been universally ousted by a colour TV adjusted by the last guest to receive nothing but rainbow stripes on all twenty-two channels. But the quiet rooms are easier to find, if you pick a suitable floor. Around the fortieth is good, raising you above direct ear-punishment from police sirens, but not high enough for helicopters to waft your window curtains. I once had a suite in Cleveland, Ohio, where even the airliners seemed to be droning around my floor looking for the airport. I could have told them they were fifteen miles off target. Still, it was snowing. But what with the noise, which at one point included a hurricane warning by mistake, the equipment having been struck by lightning, and the weather, and me due out next day on an early flight for Los Angeles, and the hotel having a pop convention which twice interrupted my quiet time with phone calls asking for Elvis Presley (in view of that last paragraph I feel I should say that this bit is true), I haven't a very clear idea what I said that evening.

One consoling feature of the suite at the Cleveland Sheraton was a large centre table in the sitting room stacked with welcoming goodies, viz., 1 bowl flowers, 1 basket fruit, 1 bottle Scotch, 1 bucket ice, 6 glasses, 12 tonics, 1 handsomely engraved card with the personal good wishes of the President of Sheraton Hotels, Inc.

I blessed his name. The loneliness of the long-distance speaker is something people should know more about. Forty floors up, 4,000 miles from home, and not a friend in the world but the bell captain who costs five dollars, you feel a warm glow, even before you've uncorked the Scotch, at a message from a man you've never met who's a mere 500 miles off in Boston, Mass.

Our link was frail, yet intricate. If I go into it a bit, keeping that Blackpool chairman ticking over in the background for a minute, it's because I don't want you to draw any false conclusions about my life-style. There exist, I believe, speakers for whom the three-room suite, wall-to-walled in ankle-clinging Aubusson, is only just good enough. Put them in anything less and they'll sue somebody. With me, it made a nice change. I spend most of my time typing in a hut in my vegetable garden, wondering whether to finish the sentence or go out and re-erect blown-down bean poles. My needs are simple. On the day of this very writing, as it happens, a strange colonel called wishing me to open a good cause at Pevensey, and found me spooning spaghetti out of a blue and white pint mug. So he soon realised that he must look elsewhere for someone acceptable to his committee. (Allowances should be made for promoters of good causes, but it's hard sometimes, when their approach lacks grace. A nearby vicar, with a church hall annex to be inaugurated, wrote: 'Having been let down at the eleventh hour, and gathering from one of my parishioners that you occasionally . . .')

My association with the President of Sheraton, Inc. began in Athens, though neither of us knew it then (and he doesn't know it even now). My wife and I got lost there. By night. With our passports, flight tickets, money and baggage left at a one night bed-and-breakfast joint whose address we didn't know, having handed it to the taximan who took us there and forgotten to get it back. It's a fairly long story. About ten minutes, stretching to fifteen if the audience has been drinking. So when I was later asked to talk for ten or fifteen minutes to a dinner of top travel men it seemed ideal material. There are, of course, people who go around making the same speech all the time, and jolly good luck to them and their thick, idle skins. The least you can do, it seems to me, is talk to bankers about banking, or lawyers about the law – hoping, all the same, to raise aspects of their subject that haven't struck them before. And if being lost in Athens, with no fixed abode and the prospect of begging in the streets, wasn't a travel subject, tell me what is.

It went so well that a gossip-writer came up afterwards and asked my name. He must have printed it, because a day or two later I was back at the bean-pole survey, coupled with the suspicion, from where I sat, that the greenhouse was falling over, when my wife brought me a letter from the London office of the *New York Times*, who had 'read somewhere' that I'd been lost in Athens. (I liked that somewhere. Trust one paper never to give another a break, even under sealed cover.) Could this be built up, as they put it, into a piece for their travel section?

Not really, I said. Once you've told about being lost in Athens, you've told about being lost in Athens, in my view – which is by no means general, considering how many people keep writing the play of the book, the film of the play, the book of the film, the TV script of the book, and the musical just around the corner. But I had, I said, recently been lost in Tunisia, an experience not yet turned into hard cash, and if they'd care for that, fine.

I thought secretly that I could, if required, do them an inexhaustible series on all the other places I've been lost in, from a television complex in Baltimore, which I finally entered up a long, sloping ramp specially put in for some elephants, to a reception at the Hyde Park Hotel.

Or the time I went to speak at the National Book League, and was told by the girl at the desk that nothing was going on there that day. I was a bit short with her. 'It just happens,' I said, 'that I've got the letter of invitation here. See? Today's date.' 'Right,' she said, handing it back, 'but if you read it again, you'll see it isn't the National Book League but the English Speaking Union.' Hard to know how these things happen. It's a good five-minute run from Albemarle Street to Charles Street, not counting stops to ask directions from policemen.

It wouldn't have mattered, but by sheer coincidence I'd got a book being published on that particular day. I don't believe in self-promotion by authors. But it had seemed naïve, even for me, to be speaking to book people, on the day you had a book coming out, without mentioning the book, and I'd asked the publishers to send round a parcel of samples to the NBL. As far as I know, it's still there, getting under people's feet. It also messed up the speech to the ESU a bit, as that was to be largely linked to the display of books which, as things turned out, wasn't there.

Disorientation at the Hyde Park Hotel was on a lesser scale. At least I got lost inside the place.

This was a Peter Scott fund-raiser for Wildlife, and other featured players included Lord Butler and the Duke of Northumberland. I sat next to an agreeable landowner. Finding during the soup that we both lived in Sussex, he gave me a lot of valuable tips on the creation of artificial lakes – he thought half an acre about the right size if you wanted to attract duck – with some mention of lawn terracing and the best plan for avenues of limes. Well, the black tie is a great leveller.

A fellow diner once found that we were both customers of the same bank. 'Awfully good people,' he said. 'I needed twelve millions to buy the [large provincial newspaper] and they couldn't have been nicer.' His wife was on my left, so at least I could stop wondering if her diamonds were real.

My friend the landowner wasn't to blame for his calm assumptions. How was he to know that I never threw my place open to the public?

But that was later.

When going out to the better class of event it's a good thing to look for the awning. Hotels tend to be rich in entrances. The one with the striped canvas is the one you want. Miss that, and you can end up among a lot of empty marble staircases. 'Where's the cloakroom?' I asked a lonely old buttons in the Hyde Park Hotel, removing my streaming coat. It was a drencher that night. 'Oh, Gawd,' he said, 'you'll never find it.' He led me on bad feet through a network of deserted corridors to a room with hat-pegs for three hundred, all unoccupied. I occupied one, washed, brushed and returned, after many misroutings, to base, where the old man was now reading a racing edition, folded down to the size of a sponge-cake. The dinner? Oh, he said, if I wanted the *dinner* . . . It meant going out again and splashing along Knightsbridge in an easterly direction until I came to an awning.

It was certainly a busier scene in there. Actual people, bustling to and fro. Hall porters. Lift lights flashing. Functionaries of indeterminate function, explaining things to Americans. Two porters, after consultation, pointed out a pair of huge closed doors. The reception. I shook the rain from my silken lapels and went in boldly.

The reception was there, all right, but they'd put me in at the wrong end of it. The room was already choked with those commandingly jewelled women and tall, clean-cut confident men who, at preliminary drink sessions, put the fear of God into speakers. Any idea that in an hour or so you'll be holding them in thrall even for thirty seconds, let alone minutes, is sheer lunacy. Their laughter is free, their chins well up, their teeth strong, white, and numerous beyond the specifications of nature. Their eyes, clear and well-opened, sweeping the room for some knight, flick past you, registering nothing. You feel the dreaded onset of Speaker's Shrivel, with its symptoms of total inadequacy, accompanied by a sense of tight clothing and a loss of height.

Ordinarily, entering a reception at the wrong end, you'd see the funny side, battle through to your host, taking him from the rear with a light chuckle, and say, 'Hello, there.

I've come in at the wrong end,' and that would be it. Paralysed by the dreaded SS, you can't make an assured move of this kind. It was in fact difficult, in that place, to make a move of any kind. It was filling up fast with all the people who'd come in at the right end. And there were more coming. Far away, on the other side of the room, I could see through the entrance doors, where tiaras and broad white shirts jostled on the stairs until such time as they should be raucously mis-announced by a man in a red coat, to receive a kind word and a handshake from Mr Scott and the Duke, and a welcoming wave into the champagne area.

Not yet being, as it were, through the Customs, I felt inhibitions about taking any champagne. I'd never needed the stuff more, and the trays bobbed all around. But it could be an embarrassment if I ever got out of my end of the room, and round and outside and on to the staircase to be almost certainly last in the queue, this being my plan at the time. People giving parties at that level wouldn't be too pleased, I imagined, to see that guests had apparently brought their private drink. I turned and butted back to the doors I'd come in by. They were locked. Belatedly, the management had closed them to traffic.

There was nothing for it but to turn again, fight through all those wedged bodies, gain my hosts, with tie askew and shoes trampled, pass between them with no word, join the queue, and presently reappear. I picked a bad moment. There was a lull when I got there. Somebody, I think, had dropped an ear-ring. My hosts' attention was momentarily free. To pass between them unnoticed wasn't on. 'It's all right,' I said, panting. 'I'm not going. In fact I'm not really here yet.' They looked baffled, and I don't blame them. Perhaps it wouldn't have mattered if they'd had time to get over it. But before I could pass down the queue, the red-coated man, who had been making vaguely helpful motions in the matter of the dropped ear-ring, looked up and got me in his sights as the next gentleman, please.

'Name?' he said. And I was in.

It was the clearing of that tricky hurdle, I think, that made me strike up an instant discourse with Lord Butler of Saffron Walden. I'd never met him, and it was mutual. His nose just happened to be the one I was reaching under to grab a passing Heidsieck. That's the way it goes, with the Shrivel. One moment you're a self-effacing midget, the next you're nine feet tall. 'And how's Oxford?' I said. Not the ideal opening for a Master of Trinity, Cambridge.

However, he later said in his speech, with a crumpled nod in my direction, 'As the editor of *Punch* has so rightly observed . . .' So, what with his never having been at Oxford, and my never having edited *Punch*, you might say we ended up quits.

There was a lecture in Pentonville. Subject, humour, and a bad choice. They'd have got more fun out of penal reform. The house was crammed, a thing which prison lecturers shouldn't feel too smug about, since it's either them or the cells. And felons aren't easy. Most audiences are drawn together by some common interest, eager to learn more about the history of the pipe-organ, or the life and times of Bishop Berkeley. With the law-breaking public,

"I THINK HE POPPED OUT TO THE NEW COMEDY AT THE ADELPHI!"

the only common denominator is that they're all in the jug. This makes it hard to hit a wave-length. Especially if the chapel acoustics are bad and your treasured throw-aways have to be belted at the high shriek.

There were other drawbacks. Having my notes on a brass-eagle lectern, from which the Bible had been removed, seemed to put a damper on any flow of comedy. I was also aware that this company, unlike others, couldn't just get up and leave. It robbed me of that minor satisfaction, which comforts a speaker in his later stages, of noticing that they were still there. I realised too late that there were things I couldn't say. Too late, that is, to think of something to say instead. 'I don't know if you've seen the new comedy at the Adelphi,' seemed hardly polite. Casual phrases about escape literature, or captive audiences, needed off-the-cuff replacements.

It would be rash to claim that it was the worst speech I ever made. Other occasions have run it close. An address in Chicago's Ambassador Hotel, say, swamped throughout by alien laughter from a public bar in the same room, open for business as usual. A luncheon at London's Savoy, paying tribute to the BBC's 40th birthday, where I planned to tell a funny story about Lord Reith, and was on my feet before I noticed him sitting three places up the table. A local Red Cross bazaar where they cued me too soon, and I harangued the backsides of the helpers as they crawled under their stalls with last-minute adjustments to the draperies, calling the while to small children and dogs. A political wine and cheese party, where the local lady Member made her farewells halfway through in a voice tuned to hounds: 'THEN I SHALL SEE YOU AT THE FORSTERS? SUCH FUN.' I finished, by contrast, in perfect silence. No offence intended. It's just that people standing with wine in one hand and cheese in the other are denied their natural implements of applause.

Still, I didn't close any of those proceedings by walking off stage into the condemned cell, as at the Ville. Handily sited within reach of holy ground, at least it was vacant, and the assistant governor hauled me out again in quick time, but it got the only laugh of the evening. Perhaps the worst was yet to come, when I was presented with an elaborate scroll of thanks, finely illuminated in three colours by a trusty from the forgery block. They told me that if I hung it in my home, well lit and at a natural break-in point, intruders would praise my name and break out again without even looking for the stamp collection. Did they take me for a fool? Any marauding Old Pentonvillian, remembering that speech, wouldn't only do the place over but set light to it on leaving as well.

It was a bemusing evening, but I remember that during question time a prisoner well down the body of the church kept shouting, 'What about Andy Capp?' and I couldn't think of an answer.

Prisoners in these pages, it occurs to me, may well be shouting what about Blackpool, Cleveland, the *New York Times*, Tunisia, the President of Sheraton Hotels, Inc., and other springboards of digression still faintly quivering. That I can answer.

Writing, then, in the *New York Times* about being lost on the trackless beaches of Hammamet, with no traces of habitation save the neat balls of camel dung and the occasional Daz packet bobbing on the tide, I described how, turning desperately inland and falling into a half-excavated swimming pool containing workmen's bicycles, I looked up to see a notice-board announcing in two languages that the Hammamet Sheraton was in course of construction there, and would be opening next summer. There was more stuff in the article than that. Even the Americans don't pay out on sixty words. But it was this passage that took the President's eye, bringing a letter of thanks for the mention, confirming the glad news on the hoarding, and inviting me to take my wife to the opening and stay on for a fortnight, all found and first-class air travel.

After a lifetime of print – granted, without introducing those brand names that keep the shrewder journalist in free holidays, malt whisky and garden cultivators – it was the first perquisite of this kind ever to come my way. Correspondence attracted by my writing leans more towards the proffered vice-presidencies of choral societies, or letters from Latin America asking if I'm the Dr Boothroyd who once treated the writer's aunt for emphysema.

I forget why, but we couldn't go to Hammamet, and regretted it. Sheratons also regretted it, but courteously programmed our names into their mailing list, and in no time at all we were being offered similar terms at the new Copenhagen Sheraton. Again we couldn't make it, and again the disappointment was mutual. In no time at all, as it seemed, the new Sheraton at, I think, Stockholm had sprung skywards, and the invitation, in gold with deckled edges, was on the mat. This time the notice was very short. A computer hiccup, perhaps. My letter of regret – they were taking some composing by now – didn't make the presidential office in time to arrest the machinery. News of waiting limousines and reception parties hurried in by every post. Scandinavian Air Services came on the phone, with deferential details of our flight and seat numbers. How little had we thought, tramping the back streets of Athens in our tattered espadrilles that time, that it would lead to this!

It didn't, in fact, lead to anything.* Either the uprush of Sheratons fell off, or they ran out of capital cities, or they have a house rule in Boston, Mass., that people who don't come three times running, stop getting asked. Plainly, however, all doors weren't closed. Learning from the public prints that Boothroyd was to visit Cleveland, the system again swung into action, thus giving me the opportunity, if anyone cares to glance back a dozen pages or so, to contrast my humble way of life, as ordinarily practised, with the brief glories of a day and a half in Ohio.

I don't know whether you're a counter. In the sense, that is, of registering the number of people in a cab queue, buttons on Underground waistcoats, seconds to fill a tea-kettle or steps up to the dentist's. In the suite of the Cleveland Sheraton I counted 3 china-cabinets, 11 chairs and

*Stop press. They finally got us to a grand opening in Bombay.

settees, 19 pictures, 2 bathrooms, 15 ashtrays, 2 television sets, 9 tables, 8 windows with gold-swagged drapes, 12 table and standard lamps, 3 telephones, 1 bed, and I may have missed something. With a few exceptions, such as the television receivers, all was in reproduction Empire of high quality, with enough gilding to do the Palace railings twice all round.

So there you are. I was only making the point that, in the speaking business, accommodation varies. Back on the UK circuit, as I recall, my first stop was Grantham. Or possibly Goole. Let's leave it loose. There, wherever it was, I took my statutory stretch-out, or quiet time, in a room with no bath, a dressing-table mirror fixed to reflect from the waist down, two men in the corridor outside crackling an ordnance survey map and discussing frontages, and someone under the window splitting beer crates with an axe and whistling the Dam-Busters' March. It was December. Neither I nor the management had a suitable meter coin for the one-bar electric fire; but at least my feet were so cold when I stepped off the bed on to a sharp door-stop that I didn't feel the blood until I got up to speak.

They said to me downstairs, during the pre-drinks, that they hoped my room was comfortable. 'Marvellous,' I said, but I knew I'd be releasing the true facts one of these days.

The trouble with speakers' hotels is that the people who book you in there have never stayed in them. Being local, they have roofs of their own to sleep under.

I forget where it was that I gave the hotel's name to the taximan and his face went blank. I guessed something, but not all. He crackled a radio query to his HQ, and even they had to look it up before he could set a course.

It was one of those places whose whole character could be deduced from its wardrobe. One door wouldn't stay open and the other wouldn't stay shut, and the knobs of the bottom drawer rested loosely in their holes, causing backward falls by guests. It seemed to be run by two large, dark girls. Neither of them manned the reception desk, which had a plate on it containing crumbs, so they took some finding, whether on arrival, when one of them finally appeared and said, 'Yes?' on a note of challenge, or later, when I came down in my dressing-gown to beg coat hangers. More delays, until a dry-cleaner's reject, painfully distorted, was exhumed from the kitchen. 'And it would be nice,' I said, still smiling pleasantly as yet, 'if I could have a waste-paper basket.' Her eyebrows went up in honest interest.

'Would it?' she said.

She wasn't trying to be funny. Just conversing. She went off for some minutes, and the other one came back. She'd be the trouble-shooter. No waste-paper basket, she said. 'You'll have to put your rubbish on the dressing table.'

The bath, a moderate walk from my room, felt rough round the water line, and had a soaked paper-back in it: eighty-six pages of strip drawings, No. 97 in Great Adventure Stories of World War Two. No bath mat. No soap. My spirits sceped away slowly, like the bathwater through its matted plug hole.

My hostess's husband – this was one of those occasions when the Ladies' Luncheon Club brought its husbands along to the annual dinner – came to collect me in a huge car and a magnificent evening shirt creation.

'Comfortable here?' he said.

Of Blackpool I remember little but the chairman. His conversation during dinner covered a lifetime of public speaking, with close details of his major triumphs, and many generous tips on delivery, audience domination, the management of notes – everything really, except how to avoid sitting next to a man who reduces your self-esteem to a hole in the ground. But I even forgave him that. I understood. A clear case of the not-to-be-outdone syndrome. I wasn't even seriously upset when he went into the *Who's Who* book-list routine.

No, what got me was his finish. He would waste no more time, he said, in introducing the speaker of the evening, because he knew . . . knew what? I prepared for flattery, which means, in my case, taking a last lungful of cigarette smoke and looking expressionlessly at the ceiling. I needn't have bothered. He wouldn't waste any more time, he said, because 'I know the ladies want to dance'.

It cracked my composure being leapfrogged like this. I opened my speech by asking the company if they'd like to dance *now*, and I think some of them, not knowing a rhetorical question when they saw one, made a move to push their chairs back. But I hastened on, rashly departing from the script, to thank the chairman for his kind words about my book that hadn't been written. So that fixed him. But then there was nothing for it but to tell the whole disgraceful story. Not a good move. Some Fleet Street spy was there, and Messrs A. & C. Black, the esteemed and vigilant publishers of *Who's Who*, must have read their press cuttings with a shock of punctured probity. When the next year's proof came round, *A Word in Public* had gone. If I couldn't bring myself to take it out, they could.

It was a great relief. The long lie nailed at last. Now, I felt, that never-written book being at last unwritten, I could write it.

I hope you follow that.

Chapter 2

Of Various Dilemmas

A guest of honour at a banquet in Thailand received a glowing address of welcome, but on rising to respond was hauled back into his seat, the response then being made by the speaker who'd just spoken already. 'Here,' explained his host, 'we employ professional orators. It's a mistake to leave speech-making to amateurs.'

Several points about that, and I'll make a couple before you do. First, it probably isn't true. They don't do this in Thailand, or, if they do, the incident never happened in this form. Telling it, as against writing it, I should either leave the whole thing much more vague – 'In Thailand,' I should say, 'or possibly Borneo, perhaps even Sumatra . . .' – or I should be comprehensively detailed: 'On the island of Tahuna in the south Pacific they have a strange but sensible custom. Some years ago, when Sir John Pilcher was our ambassador to the Philippines, he was entertained at a banquet there . . .'

The looser version would be for an audience of some sophistication, members of the Export Institute, perhaps, who might conceivably be shuttling back and forth to Thailand all the time, and would loom up at the end of the evening, eager to put me right. Diffusing the locations will confound them. They're sure about the Thais, but with Borneo or Sumatra less so.

The specific version would be for simpler, more trusting

31

folk: a Senior Wives' Fellowship, say, or the Edgware Young Women's Mizrachi Society (whose request to speak is by chance at my elbow as I write). Naturally, it's a gamble. But you'd be pretty unlucky to get Lady Pilcher among those present, particularly as her husband is now our ambassador to Japan. Oh, yes, he's a real chap all right. A speaker telling stories that aren't themselves true needs all the conviction he can get. Even for present purposes I've had to study a map of the Far East, to find a nice, pronounceable island like Tahuna after rejecting Zamboanga, Cotobato and Catanduanes; and *Whitaker's Almanack* to trace the diplomatic career of Sir John. And I thought I was in trouble there, because in the Philippines he was a mere Mister. For some reason, you can't get any fizz out of saying, 'When Mr Pilcher was our ambassador . . .' It was a stroke of luck for me that his KCMG came along and made it a name worth dropping.

Name-dropping, while we're on it, is the greatest of all stiffeners for the public anecdote, quotation or allusion.

But care is needed. In the very establishing of credibility you can destroy it. As an extreme example, a speaker who actually knows the Royal Family, either socially or professionally, may find such phrases as 'The Queen once told me,' or, 'As I was saying to the Prince of Wales,' springing to his lips. If he uses them he's in dead trouble. No actual cries of 'Liar' may rise from his audience, but the chill of disbelief does so, as thick as the mist from a Hollywood swamp. He might bring it off on rare occasions: high-powered political gatherings studded with Privy Councillors, top brass Service dinners, eminences of the horse world. It's wasted there, anyway: the Palace holds no secrets for them. You might as well try to impress a NALGO conference with a named town clerk.

If, of course, you happen to be an accredited Royal reporter, stumping the country with your talk on life as seen from the poop of HMY *Britannia*, that's different. Your stage is set in advance. Drop your references below a Marquess, and your audience feels done.

Ordinary lords aren't too bad. Again there are provisos. Even quite useful lords must be handled with care, and sometimes scrubbed altogether. 'I was talking to Lord Longford the other day . . .' Well, as it happens, you *were* talking to Lord Longford the other day, and might well want to ascribe to him, out of sheer honesty, something pretty good he said about the generation gap. But the name is too evocative. The simple, direct-drive mind of the audience, as it might be a conference of Refrigeration Engineers who've had a pretty dull three days so far, leaps instantly to Soho and Copenhagen and stirs with sly expectancy. Your cold douche on the generation gap then comes as a cruel shock, and for the next five minutes you've lost them. They go wary and suspicious. You could be leading them up some other disappointing dead end, and they're not going to be fooled this time. No. Longford will have to go. Hang whatever good thing he said on somebody else. At worst, 'A friend of mine was saying . . .' But the shine goes off it.

It's hard to find the right people to hang good things on. Luckily, most good things were said by the dead, so that's something. They aren't going to stand up at question time and floor you with corrections. But a disappointing number of good things come from nonentities, at least for name-dropping purposes. 'Ah, well,' you say, tapering off a passage, ' "Tall oaks from little acorns grow", as David Everett said.'

It shakes them, that David Everett. It shook you when you first looked it up.

'Ah, well – "one crowded hour of glorious life", as T. O. Mordaunt put it.' T. O. Mordaunt? Who ever heard of him? The man Everett could be a disc jockey, and there's glitter there, if he hadn't died, I see, in 1913; but this Mordaunt doesn't sound like a thing.

'In the immortal words of Francis Pott, Ladies and Gentlemen, "The strife is o'er, the battle done", and it only remains for me to bid the company be upstanding . . .'

It's useless. Francis Pott has killed it.

33

If you have to use their stuff, and ruin the effect with their unsung names, the only saver is to falsify the source, hang the stuff on Milton, and move quickly on.

Milton, in fact, isn't too good. He's better than Shakespeare, whose spies are everywhere, brutally familiar even with obscure bits of *Cymbeline*, but what's really wanted is instantly recognisable celebrities who aren't read much. Carlyle is pretty useful, and Proust invaluable. Any corrector likely to spot something *they* didn't say won't be in your audience anyway. He'll be out giving his lecture about Proust or Carlyle.

Be discreet, though. Don't make the attribution too wild. 'Ah, well, "Ta-ra-ra-boom-de-ay", as Marcel Proust so neatly put it', may not produce an immediate cry of, 'No, he didn't, it was Henry J. Sayers!' But they'll have that vague feeling that something's wrong, and while they're trying to work out what, they lose the drift of your story about banqueting practice in the Far East. This means that by the time they come back you appear to be plunging around in some crazy non sequitur; whereas, if they'd heard you out, they'd see how neatly you modulated from Thailand into something you want to say next.

In this case, something about the professional public speaker. Namely, that I'm one. Put it another way, I do it for money. Well, sometimes, when I don't see why I should do it for any other reason. Feel free to pale a little. I know it's a shock, and I'll try to take the caddishness out of it later. While you're recovering, there may still be a few loose ends to clear up from earlier in the chapter.

I once spoke to the Arts Theatre Club, in Great Newport Street, WC2. I throw in the occasion and the address to lend artistic verisimilitude (wasn't it Ruskin who said?) to an otherwise bald and unconvincing narrative.

It seems unlikely, looking back, that I should have done anything of the kind. There are all sorts of ways of getting into these things. This time it was for a friend.

For friends you speak free. They come into the good causes class. This is large, but ill-defined. It covers hospitals, prisons, prize-givings and general presentations, local fire brigades, dog-shows, cricket, weddings, Scouts, the United Nations, lifeboats, librarians, addresses from the pulpits of City churches and possibly, though I haven't decided yet, the Edgware Young Women's Mizrachi Society. It doesn't cover conventions, department store openings, coroners' annual dinners, or the induction of Miss Burglar Alarm, 1975.

Oddly, out of all these, speaking free for old pals is the one thing to avoid, and on at least two counts. First, your old pal is usually getting you on behalf of an old pal of his. Second, having got you, there's a fair chance that neither will show on the night. Once they have your assurance, preferably in writing, that you won't be a charge on the assets, they drop out. You may get a ring next day, asking if you enjoyed yourself. But don't bank on it. And if you're one of those mean minds that can't help an old friend, and an old friend of his, without expecting a letter of thanks, well, it serves you right for being mean-minded.

Obviously, Ladies and Gentlemen, judging by the fidgeting with necklaces, the stealthy crossing and recrossing of well-trousered knees, you don't believe any of this, and I'm sorry.

I very nearly did, in fact, get a letter of thanks after speaking at what we'll call a northern centre and save any hurt feelings. It was a smart black-tie dinner to do with the book trade, and let's leave that vague as well. It meant four hours in the train each way, and staying the night – but at least an official sought me out towards the end of the evening and said, 'Don't pay for your room, old man, it's taken care of.' When they're as nice as that you can't spoil things by bringing up your rail fare. In any case, I was getting something out of it that time. It happened that I needed an elusive book just then, and these were circles in which such items could be tracked and snared. I mentioned this to my friend (unable, unfortunately, to attend) and he said he'd see what he could do. To my surprise, he could do it. The book was there.

Back home, the letter of thanks I very nearly got turned out to be the bill.

To return to Great Newport Street, by way of the Philippines, it was an evening of general failure. Talking to actors about the theatre is as challenging as talking about it to Wednesday afternoon culture and chiropody groups in rural Sussex, if for quite different reasons. But it was relieved by a small, rare triumph. Hopelessly lost in my notes, and searching them for a navigational fix during one of those silences meant to be filled with laughter, I was blessed with an inspired ad lib. And I mean blessed. It isn't often heaven puts down its hand to touch the lips of the dumb. Revolving the folded sheet in despair, I suddenly heard myself pierce the long hush, speaking with tongues. 'Do you ever find,' I said, 'that the place you want to get to is always on the crease of the map?'

This is what we call, in the light-writing trade, recognition humour, pointing a truth that everyone knows but hasn't noticed before. I don't say this was a prime example, but it got a long enough laugh for me to find my story about Henry Irving using an off-stage drum roll to augment the applause; and I may even have gone on to ask if anyone present had brought a drum. Anyway, it meant that I got out of the place without a lynching. There were even questions, which quite often doesn't happen with me, either because my material is so exhaustive that they realise there's nothing more to learn, or so confused that they don't know what I've been on about.

One of the questions was from an agreeable actor famed on stage and screen. I forget the question, though I know I couldn't answer it. I only remember its being asked because of something that happened later.

Again, it was a theatrical occasion, on charity bent, this time. I believe it was white ties, with orders and decorations, so it must have been some years back, when I still knew where to lay hands on my Defence Medal. Also during Donald Wolfit's lifetime, because he got me into it. It was a biggish dinner, and they were all knights and CBEs but me.

Held in the hall of a City livery company, I fancy the Grocers'.

Yes. I remember toying with, but wisely rejecting Chesterton: 'God made the wicked grocer, For a mystery and a sign . . .' You toy with anything in the early stages, and at least it wasn't by T. O. Mordaunt. But it would be tough to wring a continuing argument out of. Besides, regular white-tie diners with o. and d. don't much register the venue. You can easily miss a wavelength. I once spoke to some wicked bankers in Bishop Grosseteste College, Lincoln, who hadn't heard of Bishop Grosseteste. Neither had I, before I went, but made the mistake of getting up a few witty allusions. You can rely on that old recognition humour too much. The best line with bankers is to touch lightly on the ecclesiastical and generally stained-glass atmosphere of banks, and chant them a few bars of the Bills of Exchange Act in plainsong. This usually goes well, especially if followed by an audible aside to the chairman, asking if the hall's licensed for music.

If you try that, though, be prepared for him to look worried, and send a messenger to find out.

With the affair at the Grocers' Hall I soon learnt that I had other problems. One reason why I'd said yes – apart from its always being easier than a page of fine drafting saying no – was that the Arts Theatre speech wasn't far behind me. Bad as it was, I ought to be able to salvage enough Thespiana to make a ten-minute toast response. No new thinking required. Bit of repackaging, perhaps. Throw out doubtfully authenticated stories about any giants of the theatre likely to be there. Throw in, perhaps, a few abstracts and brief chronicles of the amateur drama, such as my big moment with the sound effects for *Journey's End*, when I let them have the national anthem in the middle of act two. I began to feel confident. I might even pretend to get lost in my notes, and get off the gag about the crease of the map.

Dangerous. Let no speaker ever think that this is going to be the easy one. That never comes. What came, in this case, late as so often, was the list of speakers, that famed actor among them.

You fail to see my predicament. It was plainly impossible to deliver the material as planned, when somewhere along the table would be a man who'd heard it a fortnight before. I didn't think he would purposely wreck it, whispering to his neighbour, 'You're going to hate this next bit', or 'He always tells that one', though from what came afterwards I shouldn't have been so sure. I might have told myself that actors, of all people, think nothing of making the same speech a thousand nights running, if they run that long. But it would have made no difference. The words were staled on my lips.

There was something else. I now saw for the first time that there were to be ten toasts proposed, each with two responders. You have to hand it to those who dine for charity. They can certainly take punishment. The speakers' names were lustrous. I still don't know, and never shall now, why Wolfit thought of me, with all that talent around, though it wouldn't be the first time I've been confused with Lord Boothby.* However, there I was, and down as the second responder to the tenth and last toast of the evening.

Well, consider.

There are pros and cons about speaking after meals, as against cold, teetotal addresses in drill halls. Among the pros, obviously, are the well-fed, half-stewed and indulgent listeners. Though this doesn't apply, it should be noted, to after-breakfast speaking. I've only done this once, and learnt my lesson. Sunday morning, it was, at a Writers' Summer School in Derbyshire, and I was first out of the trap, 9 a.m. sharp. I didn't realise why all the front rows were empty, and students who couldn't get into the back ones were bunched around the exits. I, at least, had had the

---

* After his successful action against a Sunday paper I got a letter addressed, 'Sir Basil Boothby, Editor of Punch, House of Lords, London', asking me to pass on a piece of the damages. Check your facts, I always say.

sense not to eat prunes at breakfast. Others had been less cautious. Traffic near the doors was constant.

A drawback in addressing the wined and dined is that you're usually one speaker among many. There are hazards here. For one thing, you can't rely on those who go before not to pre-explode your best gags. Ideally, of course, your material should guard against this by rejecting the obvious. Speaking to bankers, you can safely take it that others will handle the overdraft joke. To lawyers, don't bother to look up Shakespeare to see just where he said the law was an ass (interesting if you do, though, because it was actually Dickens). To advertising men, you can leave it to a co-speaker, if not several, to say, 'Sweet are the uses of advertisement'. But sometimes the field is narrow, and the references obvious and few. Service reunions, should you be caught by one in a weak moment, get through the small common fund of anecdotes in no time; if you're low on the bill, you can delete from your notes, one by one, the time when Titchy Westlake . . . when Lofty Coote . . . when Dodger Cagthorpe and Dingy Beeston – Good God! don't say he's even telling the one about the CO's dog and Crafty Carstairs.

Speakers unable to switch their script suffer horribly as their time draws nigh. If they can't think of anything better – and many can't – than to complain, with a hollow attempt at breeziness, that all their best gags have been pinched, and then re-tell them with pedantic amendments of plot and character, my advice is to fall sideways from their chairs with a loud cry, when willing hands will carry them out.

You can also get an extra shot of brandy that way.

Though this isn't exactly what happened to me at the Grocers' Hall, it was near enough to ruin my evening. The actor spoke before me. So did everyone else, come to that. But he's the one that sticks, because he used my crease-of-the-map routine, believe it or not. He didn't, of course, lose his place in his notes, but only pretended to. So it wasn't an ad lib, either, but only a pretended ad lib. It didn't go too well, and there are subtleties here. It had saved me at the

Arts Theatre through audience sympathy and relief. They'd seen me teeter at the abyss, and recover when all seemed lost. They had rejoiced with me. Audiences, for all their faults, don't enjoy a speaker's discomfiture. But at the Grocers' Hall the speaker's discomfiture, being merely contrived as a springboard for the crack, failed to get across.

If it did raise a laugh or two, none of them came from me. How could this man, agreeable and civilised by all accounts and appearances, in whose single interest I had abandoned a whole speech and slaved through the small hours to devise a new one, actually stand up there pinching the stuff? It wasn't as if he'd just happened to pluck from the general hatful some joke I'd planned to use. This is bad luck, but it happens. I knew that the crease of the map was original with me. It appeared in none of the manuals of oratory entitled 'Laughter and Applause', 'Louder and Funnier', 'A thousand and one Humorous Stories for the After Dinner Speaker', and the like. But I suppose what really threw me was the blow to my ego, at a time when that was the last thing it needed. All the speakers, it was to be assumed, had also had a list of the others. My name would be in it. The flagrant filcher of the map gag obviously didn't know where he'd got it from. I had made no personality impact at the Arts Theatre Club. I was a cipher, and again due to appear as one, a talking hole in the wall, in about fifteen minutes time.

Distracting, these reflections. The speaker must only think of his speech, as pilots at take-off know nothing but their own headphones and the waiting waste of runway. This is why, in the hideous lull before clearance, he bends his waxen grin on his neighbours long after their funny stories have passed their point: or sometimes goes the other way, giving a shrill laugh as the Lord Lieutenant's lady tells of a nasty accident to a favourite uncle.

Concentration was further diffused that night by an impulse to chuck out the new speech and use the old one after all. It seemed improbable, from recent evidence, that Mr X's sensibilities would be outraged. If he hadn't associated me with it last time, and now dimly recognised some of it, he would only think I'd pinched it from some other chap we'd both heard somewhere. I decided, in the last wild, yawing moments, to stand firm. For one thing, I could have forgotten some of the old stuff. If so, there was no falling back on the map creases this time. He had seen to that. For another – and I felt a slight sizzle of advance relish, immediately suppressed, over-confidence being a mocker – the new stuff was to end with a device which, as far as I knew, had never been worked before.

My idea was to frighten them. Rising at 11.30 or thereabouts, the last speaker of the evening, I would remind them that I alone stood between them and their beds, but had no intention of abandoning a syllable of my prepared material.

It felt promising. The words rolled richly.

'You will appreciate,' I said, 'Mr Chairman, my lords, ladies and gentlemen, that you are entirely in my power. The hour is late. Many of you have far to go. You are anxious to return to your architect-designed residences in the foothills of the Berkshire Downs. Your hired limousines, now assembled outside this historic Hall, are ticking up the ducats. For myself, I happen to have a bed just round the corner, a matter of a minute's walk. My engagement book for tomorrow is blank. I have a great many stories to tell you, all extremely long . . .'

I could see it working. And the success of something new is one of the few satisfactions of this strange business. Here and there a distinguished face paled. Glances were exchanged, watches consulted, at first with stealth, then in open alarm. It could happen. I could mean it. The early laughter, mild but indulgent, tailed off nervously. After three or four minutes the whole company was stricken and still.

Then I let them off the hook. On second thoughts, I said, I'd do the decent thing. The toast having already been adequately dealt with by the previous responder [Emlyn Williams, a hard man to follow], I would now, after all, sit down. Goodnight. Thank you for having me. And you can all go home.

It went very badly. There should have been a great up-rush of relieved applause. No such thing.

This was because, as I presently learnt from the toast-master, the evening's high spot was now due. Eight turns on the stage which everyone knew about but me. Mighty theatrical names giving their talents for nothing, who had whiled away the long, long night in the wings, only to hear, from some idiot and would-be wit who hadn't read the back of his menu, that they had apparently been wasting their time.

Chapter 3

Artful Aids

Speak first, drink later, is the recommended order. But hard to arrange. As the long night closes, it isn't only the diners who want to go home, but the waiters. Only the speaker, in fact, wants to stay a little. His work done, he feels himself turning back into an ordinary human being, with ordinary human appetites, such as hunger and thirst. The hunger isn't serious, just a hollow pang of regret for the dishes he couldn't bear to look at, let alone eat, an hour before. But the thirst bites at his windpipe, and the waiters have gone. All evening they've been filling glasses you daren't empty, and they've gone too.

To drink first is tempting, but dangerous. You may not be able to speak later. It's a delicate course to steer, between stone sober tongue-clacking dread, your notes trembling out of vision like lawnmower handles, and that giddy exaltation in which you hear yourself, as in an echo-chamber, gabbling a heap of old rubbish.

Tongue-clacking, perversely enough, can happen in drink as well as out of it, particularly if you timidly submit to the standard pourings, which tend to be wines, instead of boldly shocking everyone by a demand for iced water instead. Wine, that maketh glad the heart of man, Psalms 104, 15, also drieth the lips. This means ruined timing and lost laughs – and so no chance to take a leisurely moistener during the natural breaks. It's one thing to do this to accompanying laughter, quite another in the teeth of a silent company, when your frenzied gulps puncture the hush like gongs.

I strongly commend the iced water. It's a question of getting it. You can't start campaigning too early. Put it to the chairman even as you sit. You will need, you tell him, a glass of iced water when you rise to speak. 'No trouble there,' he says, once he's checked that you're serious. He then turns to the lady on his left, saying what sad news it is about Charlie Bingham or some other absent friend. The white wine arrives. Oh, well. Not to be a nuisance, lay off until after the soup. Then, 'Did we have any luck with the iced water?' 'Ah,' he says. 'We'll get on to that right away.'

But somehow we don't. The fish comes and goes. You feel like a bore. This man is going to remember you, if at all, as the victim of a weird obsession. Never mind. 'Iced water?' you say again as the chops appear, and with them the claret. But the cutlery is in full clash by now, and he doesn't quite catch it. 'You did? That's very interesting.'

By the time the port comes round you know you're on your own. You seize the waiter and put it to him. 'Getting it now, sir.' But you can tell he'd say the same if you'd asked for a gallon of paraffin. The pattern of public dinners, if not in fact computerised, is just as inflexibly predestined. All will go well as long as some wild eccentric doesn't want an apple, or no mashed potato with his sole Lydia. Or, as it might be, some iced water.

And by now this really is getting to be obsessive. You know it, and you can't help it. Time is passing. You haven't been drinking, and you're dry. Certainly you daren't drink the port, finest of all wines for gumming the tongue like a luggage label. In ten minutes you'll be up there, trying to get out your 'Mr Chairman' and only managing a 'Miktek Chekmuk'.

If the water comes in time – and it's been known, a reprieve when all seemed lost – there's often trouble over a suitable container. The punched cards, at this time of the evening, might still run off a liqueur glass, but nothing on any scale for slaking. If by a miracle they do find something bigger, it's enormous, standing a foot above the table. Remember to keep your gestures small.

Usually, if it comes at all, not only your own but everybody else's speeches are over by then. 'You wanted some iced water, sir?' says the last surviving waiter, bringing it.

At least he's got his tenses right.

It's before the meal that your hosts are liberal with the liquor. They know it as the great loosener of tongues. So during the gay run-up, foreshadowed on the invitation by the dread 7.30 for 8 (or, even dreader, 6.30 for 7.30), they like to get as much stuff into you as they can. Watch it. Not knowing the difference between loosened tongues and floating teeth, it's surprising the risks they take. There must be speakers, it's true, who only hit cruising speed at the fifth deep Scotch. Others are in overdrive on a small mild-and-bitter.

Americans, on public occasions, tend to go the other way, surprising in the very cradle of Alcoholics Anonymous. They put all speakers in the weak-headed class, and deprive them accordingly. Perhaps they've had bad experiences, with guests of honour helped to their feet when performance time comes, only to crash at once into the flower arrangements. Certainly there's a strong residual whiff of Prohibition in their TV and radio studios. The BBC has her faults. But even today, under conditions of stern budgetary restraint, she still clanks in with her medicinal trolley before the event, and wrings a chaser out of the duty officer's bar after it. Broadcasters in the States are lucky to see anything but a midget paper cup of water.

This matters less on vision than on sound. With TV you're likely to be on and off at high speed, and a summoning of natural adrenalin is enough for the five minutes' lens-beaming before collapse sets in. But those late night radio chats can be real dry times. Two hours, just you and an ashtray.

To be fair, parched in Minneapolis once, on KMSP-TV, I was given a soft-boiled egg. It was a breakfast-time show.

They may have thought it helped with the atmosphere. Obviously there's something immoral about large Martinis at that time of day. But an egg in a coffee-cup, eaten with a spoon, is no booster into top sparkle.

Cicero, who was rich in warnings to orators, including the risk of audience distraction by unsightly toga folds, had nothing on alcohol. I don't know what drinks were on offer around 70 BC by, say, the Philippi Chamber of Trade. This would in itself have been interesting. More so, any Ciceronian tips on how much and when. When, particularly. Those liberal hosts of some nineteen centuries later often overlook an elementary fact, that the speaker's alcohol level, be it pumped never so affably high between the 7.30 and 8, can only go one way after that, which is down. Even a man who foolishly takes the subsequent table wines, as programmed, feels a general ebbing.

With short-term affairs it doesn't matter. The modest scale of injection at the straight lecture in the civic centre, where you arrive a few minutes before H-hour to be launched on a wavelet of ratepayers' sherry, the bottle then being locked in a green steel cupboard, is enough, just, to give the required slight edge over the abstaining audience, silently bundled up in its overcoats on stackable municipal chairs. Provided no time is lost on surprise preliminaries, the summer outing plans, perhaps, or a tribute to some good friend of the society recently deceased – you inevitably get this sometimes, and it's a real challenge to modulate into your performance, billed in the vestibule as 'The funniest evening of the year' – or a grindingly long introduction from one of those chairmen who feel that it's really their evening rather than yours . . . provided you're spared all this, the single preliminary shot will still have a bit of mileage in it by the time you take the stand.

But I have before me, as I write, the impending programme for a Golden Jubilee Dinner in Lancashire. My lecture agency's briefing slip, among other details (availability of pianos, projectors and microphones, length of speech required, distance from railway station to hall), had said 7 for 7.30. With luck, it looked to me as if I should be on my feet by 8.30, tucked up in bed by 10.

But the organisers have now been thoughtful enough, as they often aren't, to send their official running order. It contains twelve items, ending with me. I see that I'm timed for 10.15. A long hard night.

As to drink, this could be a tough one. At 6.30, not 7, it suggests here, the booze will start to flow. Not that I'm fooled any longer by these timetables. The more rigid and detailed their information, the more they disintegrate on the due day.

The pre-drinks may start on time, and indeed before. It's as the evening wears on that things become loose. If I'm up and doing at this Jubilee a minute before 10.45 I shall be surprised and delighted.

Four hours poised for the spring will mean nice judgement. Even spreading the intake thin, and hiding every other glass among the goodies on the raffle table, could mean reaching peak potential halfway through dinner. This happens. And the President's lady, after you've rocked her through seven courses with wit and humour, is plainly mystified when you at last unfold your aching back and produce an exhausted monotone with stumbling at difficult words. Especially if her own table-talk has been sparse, causing you to keep things bright by leaking the speech's high spots. To use them at the appointed place is then hopeless. Dead fireworks.

Yet to lay off until later can mean (a) throwing the organisers into despondency, fearing they're lumbered with a teetotaller who will fail, when the test comes, to catch the spirit of the occasion, or (b) going wild in the last few minutes and alarming them in the opposite direction. A guest of honour who has waved everything aside all night, and now suddenly demands a triple vodka, is obviously some kind of nut they've got hold of. Or worse: he's been on the medically prescribed wagon for months and has chosen this of all moments to jump off.

Or there are pills.

47

I'm not often on the pill. But there are times. Also timings. And choices, between a bracer-upper, because you were at the Café Royal last night and since then you've had to get to Stockport,* and a calmer-downer, because you've only just looked at the organisers' fixture list and noticed that their last two speakers were the Lord Chief Justice and Spike Milligan.

It's a hard decision, if you have to face it. Either pill can ease the pain; the bracer by honing your persona to a fine edge, so that you take the occasion by storm, all floodgates of wit, grace and gallantry flying open, from the clamour of the ante-room, where dignitaries' wives and sweethearts blossom like flowers as you stream out your fulsome flatteries, to the speech itself, brilliantly updated with spontaneous local references and spiced with inspired asides – is this all self-delusion? If so, you don't care.

The calmer-down, on the other hand, anaesthetises the nerve ends, and can go too far in this. True, you don't worry about falling below the high standards set last year by leaders in the field, and that's good. Less good is to find yourself reflecting, as the toast-master screams your name, that you don't give a damn whether you talk to these people or not, whoever the hell they are.

But in either case, timing is all. Medicate too soon, and you could be snoring on your feet. Too late, and the guests are collecting their cloaks just when you're ready to lead the community singing.

For this reason, the disrupted timetable can wreck everything. Organisers who greet you cheerfully with the news that arrangements have been put back an hour, on a snap decision to open the proceedings with musical selections, say, by local artistes, don't understand why their speaker's smile should drop from his face like snow off a roof. How should they? He alone knows the awful truth: that he's taken his pill, and that deep in his system an irreversible chemistry is at work. He is now to come on at ten instead of nine? The fascinating raconteur, as billed, will in the

* You're a fool. Space out those reckless acceptances.

event turn out a simpering loon, who sits down twenty minutes early without even proposing the toast.

What happens, I wonder, to those timetables? They look all right. Why do they always have to fall apart like a do-it-yourself bookcase?

Luncheons aren't so bad. Even today, with the twenty-hour week an affirmed sociological dream, there are still people who like to get back to their desks in the afternoon. Enticed into membership of a luncheon club that tops off its business with a talk, they make it clear on enrolment that they'll be leaving at 2.15 sharp or else. This drives Hon Secs to get the speaker on his feet at 1.45, even if he still has a piece of celery sticking out of his mouth.

The talk untrammelled by gastronomics of any kind is equally manageable. You mount the podium on the dot, the chairman proclaims your name and subject, if known*, and you're all right. Anyone can time a large gin, or even a small pill, in such ideal conditions.

But dinners, no.

Since I mentioned that Lancashire Golden Jubilee a page

---

* Chairmen can get confused, especially when these rites occur weekly. 'Mr Hurstwood on tropical fish?' said one of them in a preliminary whisper to a friend of mine named Gibbs, whose subject was roses.

49

or two back, the occasion has come and gone. I had allowed in my mind, you may remember, for a half-hour lag between the advertised and actual time of performance. I was well out.

I rose, in fact, seventy-five minutes late, which meant, even with ruthless cutting and stitching, and the ruination of all passages needing a bit of elbow room to be effective, that I was still going at ten minutes after midnight, with the bar well closed, the vote of thanks still to come, and a seven o'clock train in the morning.

I look back with some pride. Had I taken the timetable at its word, disaster would have been inevitable. By speech time, all aids to audience mastery would have worn off, leaving a mere shrivelled nut rattling about behind my frothing jabot. (The return of frills for men is a boon for the after-dinner speaker with a galloping pulse rate; in the era of the soft, plain front, studs could visibly tremble, like tiny golf tees in a high wind.) But experience tells.

A glimpse into the room reserved for the president's private reception alerted me to the likely course of events. Things had obviously got off the mark early. Un-English embraces were being exchanged – it was one of those all-male reunion occasions, where everyone has known everyone else for twenty-five years, and the speaker, hovering in the doorway in the hope of being approached by the man he's been corresponding with for weeks, but who isn't there, quickens with sympathy for the soldier who turns and runs.

The decibel count was high. If this merry company, I said to myself, was going to file in to the top table at 7.30, as laid down, my name was Harriet Beecher Stowe. It was already 8.20 when the photographers arrived. They're always good for half an hour, by the time they've herded selected celebrities into waxwork groupings, ordered them to point at things, paused to adjust wayward chains of office, loosed off the mandatory number of dud flash bulbs, and then restarted the whole show from scratch because the president, a man of impeccable local standing, finds he's gone on record with a glass in his hand.

We filed in at 8.55. Eighty-five minutes down.* The delay, someone said, was with the approval, or at least the assent, of the banquet staff, who'd had troubles of their own, but it would have been all the same, very probably, if they hadn't. Something had forewarned me that it was a pill night. If things had gone to plan, it would have been about now that I swallowed it. I fingered it in my pocket and postponed indefinitely. The other speakers, timed in my briefing at a total of ninety minutes, hadn't been noticeably conserving their sobriety up to this point, and weren't likely to start now, in my judgement. I could up all that lot by a half, I decided during the fish.

During the duck, I saw that these figures might be open to revision, as the toastmaster began demanding that various visiting contingents should take wine with the chairman (I once used to think that he paid for all those drinks), which is a fair old time-waster, once the cheering and banter have had their fling. The loyal toast, unexpectedly with musical honours, further delayed the deadline. The interval, optimistically allotted twenty minutes, would of course run to thirty. Even your most diligent usher, barking like a sheep-dog and striking the guests with knouts, can't hope to clear the wash-room of elated reminiscers in less.

It was in the wash-room that I took my bracer-upper. It wasn't only that I estimated about an hour in hand before speaking, but I should need all my resources to entertain, in the manner to which they were accustomed, a company extremely drunk, armed in some cases with mechanical devices simulating laughter when squeezed, and exchanging, amid the sanitary-ware, stories of horrific blueness.

Again my estimate was out. But the other way, this time. The chairman, nudged into a belated sense of responsibility by messages saying people were sorry but had to leave for their last trains, suddenly eliminated a clutch of items – including a roll-call of delegations which should have been

* It happened, as a matter of interest, to be the day when Apollo 17 landed on the moon, eight seconds late.

good for forty minutes – cut his own speech to the bone and introduced mine in twelve words flat.

My pill and I were properly caught out. I began the speech, I remember, with all the sluggishness of a man drained by five hours' unremitting jocundity among four hundred total strangers. Then Messrs Burroughs, Wellcome seeped into the bloodstream and saved the day. Or the night. The day, in fact. It isn't often (thank God), that you can end an after-dinner speech by bidding the company good morning.

Chapter 4

There and Back

Somewhere in Israel there's a tree planted for me. I came across a certificate, the other day, saying so. And a nicer present, in lieu of fee, I can't think of. I hope it's doing useful work, but I haven't seen it, and don't know whether it's bearing oranges, shading donkeys, or merely oxygenating the air.

This was some time ago, and it should have a few rings on its trunk by now. I was speaking to a Jewish youth organisation in deepest Whitechapel. I can't think why, particularly as it was a Sunday morning, and Sussex to Whitechapel, by Sunday train and bus service, isn't a thing to take on lightly.

All I remember is the journey back, or part of it. A lady helper on the coffee and biscuits side offered me a lift to Victoria in her car. My instinct, I remember, was to decline, not so much because of her L-plates – she blamed them, unasked, on a learner daughter – as of the energy-drain of light, gay talk with strangers in confined spaces. This is taxing enough before a speech, but the need to convince at least yourself that you're light and gay, on the chance that the momentum will finally get you up on your feet in the same mood, keeps you merrily a-chatter. After, however, it's harder to rise to it. You think enviously of puppets. On curtain fall they get thrown into a box, and the lid slams, and they don't know how lucky they are.

Still, there was a train I might catch by private transport which I couldn't hope to make by bus. Attracted by the bonus of getting home for late lunch instead of early tea, I graciously accepted.

All went well, if a little wobbly, until we approached Puddle Dock. It was a small, hard-riding car, needing firm hands at the wheel, and only a fool would have distracted the driver's attention with reminiscence, anecdote and quip. But silence on the part of others only makes me talk for two. It happens notably on the telephone to broadly desked executives or other persons of unassailable self-sufficiency. Their conversation is so strung out with silences that I'm impelled to say everything twice, and keep breaking off to ask if they're still there, which seems to annoy them.

My driver wasn't one of these. If she didn't say much it was probably because of her preoccupation with a periodic clutch roar and a whimsical selection of traffic lanes. She may not even have heard how I was mistaken for the Duke of Bedford outside the National Portrait Gallery, or became separated, in a Mexican dust storm, from my guided tour of the Toltec temples of Teotihuacán – a long one, that, and it advanced the journey well into Upper Thames Street. So it wasn't necessarily my fault that we then ran under the back end of a stationary cement-mixer outside the Mermaid theatre. I felt, all the same, that in view of her kindness, and piteous speculations on what her husband would say, I could hardly regard our association as ended, and slip down the nearby Blackfriars tube.

It took time and waning charm, persuading men from a demolition site in Trig Lane to free our wheels with crowbars. My driver's insistence, this done, on continuing the journey as promised, did nothing to ease things. There are times, and there are not, for a passenger to go on sparkling. We continued as two dumb strangers, our muscles – well, I speak for myself – bunched with tension, and we parted with minimum formalities, to meet again by post only: sympathy and regret on my side, copy correspondence from the insurance company on hers.

None of it was anybody's fault. Not even my being plunged by the delay into a festival of mainline track maintenance, a regular Sunday event on British Rail. It meant all change at East Croydon, and a long loop by Southdown bus to Three Bridges. My wife, when I at last reeled in for an early supper, placed the blame equally on Jewish youth, for letting me in, and me for letting myself be let. Even the news that a tree with our name on was to flourish in some sunny kibbutz didn't bring her round entirely.

Dodge the weekends is a sound principle. Grimsby or Hull on Friday evening means return travel on Saturday morning, or even afternoon. This is bad enough, what with every convenient train carrying the dread timetable symbol 'E' (see page 3, 'Mondays to Fridays'), and all the others a confusion of signal repairs, loud, jolly families and football supporters.

Sundays are worse. While your audience of the night before are sprawling in bed with the papers, forgetting you've ever been there, you're the only living thing on the platform of Manchester, Piccadilly, sitting on a hard bench outside the closed refreshment room, the rails stretching bleak and empty in all directions. I sat thus at Retford one still Sabbath, and had an eerie feeling, in the hush, that there was a message for me. It turned out to be behind my back, on a hoarding that said 'Inter-City Makes the Going Easy (and the Coming Back)'. In an area of white paper foolishly left vacant by the designer, someone had neatly scripted:

I DIED HERE

Over-dramatic, possibly, compared with the brave last words of Captain Oates, but the acceptance of doom was there all right.

On a recent February Sunday in Southport, had you been strolling in the drizzling gale between the grey horses of the distant sea and a statue of Queen Victoria, apparently in lead, gazing unmoved on a shuttered bingo hall and other joyless enticements of resorts out of season . . . the huts

water-logged in salt pools, no guide to their holiday function save the words PAY HERE . . . the boarded-up stalls,
still bravely advertising hats, pies, belts, balloons, buckets
and spades and fresh-cut balm cake . . . had you been, as I
say, strolling there − well, more fool you, that's the first
thing: the second is that you might have seen another figure
doing the same, pausing now and again to stir with his
drenched shoe the pages of a sodden hi-fi catalogue, or aim-
lessly try the door of a locked Gents', a figure hunched to
the scalp in its overcoat, blown this way and that by the
fiercer gusts, moving with a sort of intent purposelessness
to a point where the pavingstones end in trackless dunes,
and the walker can only turn round and come back, and
then, butting head down against the now shuttered Tunnel
of Love, turn yet again, with a glance at his watch showing
still three and a half hours to train time . . .

Would you believe, watching him, that − ? Oh, you've
gone home, and I don't blame you. Put it another way,
then, you'd hardly take this man for last night's majestic
speaker at the Prince of Wales hotel, itself now somewhat
subdued in the mid-morning twilight and the bars not open
yet. He is muttering to himself, at the risk of the sou-
westerly getting into his mouth and blowing his teeth out.
He speculates glumly on how he came to say yes to a Saturday night, without checking that the first diesel for the
south isn't due out until half-past two, and that only marked
with a 'b' for 'buffet'.

He could, it's true − oh, let's abandon this device − I
could, it's true, have lunched at the hotel. But I was seized,
as always, with post-speech insecurity, a social tremulous-
ness. Strange, indeed, that the man who last night homed
in on the top table with all the unconcern of an IBM, and
kept eight hundred eyes open for an hour and a quarter,
now doubts his ability to front up a brusque waitress, such
as it would be just his fate to get today. Besides, I wasn't
yet in the mood to eat. The prospect of having to change
at Crewe, nay, perhaps at Wigan also, lay heavily on my
appetite.

I had time on my hands. The effect of this on hotel dining-rooms, in my experience, is to produce the quickest meal in the history of catering, four courses in fifteen minutes flat, and the coffee banged down before you've even tinker-tailored your plum stones. Leave it until time's short, on the other hand, and it can take an hour, with pauses between courses that you could read *War and Peace* in, while the staff, in groups behind a screen, hiss at each other in some private dispute. Besides, to eat alone, as all speakers know who are left over from the night before, is to get the little table next to the service doors, the one they throw the spare cutlery on. The breeze from the waiters' coat-tails, as they dart to some other, always some other, table, blows up the corners of your tiny tablecloth into the soup, and your pepper and salt are often snatched up in passing, to meet a more prestigious demand from a table in the window.

I plumped for the buffet car this time. A wrong decision. At Liverpool, Exchange, there was an unusual notice on the barrier blackboard, 'Regret no catering facilities on

REGRET NO CATERING FACILITIES ON THIS TRAIN DUE TO VANDALISM.

this train due to vandalism.' The sort of story you'd like to hear more about, really, and quite a collector's piece for connoisseurs of railway regrets, if not quite a match for a favourite of mine at Paddington once: 'Services subject to cancellation and delay owing to body on line.' Where's the consideration, these days? I was made late by that for a literary luncheon in Taunton, and had a struggle with my good-taste angel all the way down, debating whether to work it into the response for the guests.

If you're wondering why I was at Liverpool, Exchange, after all those seafront apprehensions about Wigan and Crewe, I was a little surprised myself. I'd found at the last minute that Sunday's trains took a different route from Saturday's, owing to similar fine calculations, I suppose, to those ABC entries that send you panicking to the code key, to see what's meant by an ominous asterisk, and it only says, '*1 min. earlier Thursdays'. I was lucky to discover the Sunday alteration, in a way, because I'd had wild thoughts, passing the grey Southport hours, of taking a cab to Wigan, damn the expense, and cutting out the two-coach local dawdler, resting on its laurels at Birkdale, Ainsdale, Freshfield, Formby, Hightown, Hall Road; Blundellsands and Crosby, Seaforth and Litherland, Marsh Lane and Strand Road; Bootle, Bank Hall and all stations to No Purpose, as it would have turned out.

In another way I was less lucky, because on the Sunday route, getting from Lime Street, Liverpool, to Exchange, Liverpool, with not much time but a large bag in hand, and no hint of a cab except a whitewashed TAXIS in an empty rectangle, is a cause for mounting alarm. As the minutes slide by, you decide to abandon the bag in the forecourt and seek help in the broad, deserted shopping street where there's no sign of life but the heavy clang of the traffic lights changing, and your only hope is to telephone a car-hire firm by courtesy of the reception desk of the Grand Hotel, whose doors prove to be bolted and barred, and no reception desk inside, either, when you come to peer through the ageless dust of the glass panels. And it doesn't help, sprinting back to the taxi rank, to see that your bag's gone – though it's only that a man in a full-skirted raincoat is standing there, blocking it from view.

'You waiting for a cab?' I said to him, for once ready to assert precedence. 'No,' he said. It seemed a funny way to spend a Sunday afternoon.

So I dragged the bag into the street and at last flagged down a lonely car. I'd had time to rehearse my story. I was a Special Branch man whose wife had collapsed on Exchange station, having rushed me a message by a member of the uniformed branch who had then been unfortunately called away to a murder. Some murders, perhaps. Give it all the credibility you can.

On second thoughts, need I be a Special Branch man *and* have a collapsed wife? People have human feelings. Perhaps if I just – However the car turned out to be a taxi, which I hadn't realised in the fine rain now falling. The London idea of having recognisable shapes, even at long range, has much to be said for it. I once rushed down the steps of an art gallery in Detroit into the back seat of a traffic-snarled Yellow Cab, and the driver, a middle-aged lady, started hitting me with her handbag. It was in fact a yellow private car. They get nervous about that sort of thing in America's major cities.

So there it was, for Southport, and if my hosts had dropped me a line asking if I got home all right I could have put their fears at rest. You usually do get home all right. Or home, anyway. It's just that you feel, for a day or two, that you'll never be the same man again.

They don't often drop a line, not after the event. This is probably a good thing. You'd feel impelled, in answer to their kind enquiry, to give them an account of the homeward journey, still fresh in your mind. Tedious for them, and a waste of useful material for you. With the passage of time, and emotion recollected in tranquillity, even you will see what a lark it was, sitting around Liverpool airport in that Stygian upstairs bar, or standing on Reading station, long after your due arrival time at Oxford, while British

Rail sent to Paddington for a new fuse for their blown-out diesel. Ideal stuff, this, when next you can't think of anything to say to the Chairman's lady during the sherry trifle. Or you might get it into a book some time.

When I last sat in the artificial gloaming at Liverpool airport I was bleeding from the scalp, a reward for being over-conscientious. The connecting flight being an hour late, I'd thought it only polite to telephone the Isle of Man Ladies' Luncheon Club, who were waiting to meet me at Ronaldsway. Man at one of the check-in desks, after some consideration, led me behind the scenes, and I sent a message under the Irish Sea. I took a short cut back, which involved a jaunty hop on to the luggage platform between two desks, adding a cubit or thereabouts to my stature, and thus dealing some sort of hanging signboard a fearful blow. Airline staff came running. But it was all right, the thing wasn't seriously damaged.

The incident inevitably made a talking point at the lunch. It takes thicker hair than mine to hide a new pink plaster. The lady at the next soup plate, after sympathetic enquiries, went on to take a strong line about the generally unsatisfactory nature of air travel. I said, well, yes, but it still had advantages over those awful boats. She disagreed, but with the gentleness of true breeding, and explained that her husband owned the boats. You can't be too careful. It's lucky she was nice.

But they all were, that time. They often are. More often than not? Probably. I don't know. What is it that the sun-dials say. Something about only recording the sunny hours. Good for you, sundial. But most of us, perversely, remember the days when the clouds rolled up, and we waited in the rain for the car that didn't. This happened to me outside a new station somewhere. I seem to think of Essex. Its concrete lamp standards were still strung with wet bunting, celebrating the inaugural visit of Mr Richard Marsh in person, and there was a dead cat on the line, which school children were discussing with interest. This melancholy display, with the non-arrival of the car, made me feel sad and lonely, and an object of curiosity, later of pity, to the station staff. Or did I imagine that? Of course. A man who is obviously stood up, as the cars come and go, none of them for him, though hope springs afresh with each arrival, to die with each departure, must think himself pitiable even if no one else does.

After an hour I telephoned. I would have done it before, but I needed time to work up the brightness, prepare a few cheery rebuttals of apology from the other end. One thing, I could congratulate myself on having brought the telephone number, even though I had to squat on the floor of the booking hall and dredge it from the bottom of my overnight bag. Always take the relevant documents. A golden rule. Not only for telephone numbers – call-box directories suffer terribly, and if you want a Mrs Dyson you can find all the pages gone up to Elliot – but for useful little forgotten PS's in the early correspondence . . . husbands will be there on this occasion . . . or the Bishop . . . could you refer in your speech to the society's work for footpath preservation? . . . the meal will be cooked and served by school-leavers from the local domestic science class, whose teacher will be sitting on your right . . .

Working up the brightness wasn't necessary with the Essex lady, as she had enough for two, and went off into peals of laughter. It was the twenty-four hour clock, she said. She'd been thinking 16.20 was twenty past six. Funny, because she was wondering if I hadn't left it a bit late, with the dinner at half-past seven. Never mind. These things were sent to try us. She'd be with me in no time. It was typical of her, she said, and the girls would scream when they heard about it.

Half an hour later the red mini rocked to a halt. However, I'd registered 'in no time' as an elastic expression, and had learnt, after showing her address to the ticket inspector, that she lived fifteen miles off.

Wasn't it awful, she said, still laughing. Just a sec, and she'd move the dog on to the back seat. She had to drop him off at the kennels. They were going to Spain in the morning. 'I'm a sun-worshipper,' she said. Had it been raining when I left home? What did I think of Colchester (or possibly Braintree)? She hoped I'd enjoy the evening. Last month they'd had Enoch Powell (or possibly Patrick Moore), who were terrific, and she couldn't remember whether she'd warned me about the bad acoustics.

First contacts can set the key. Speakers can't be choosers. If they could, would they rather have this, and feel reduced to a numb inadequacy, or, as often happens, a dragooned husband at the wheel, plainly weighed down by the events in prospect. How many more like him, you wonder, as you chat in a manly way about brake-fluid, humouring their wives at this annual turn-out? And what chance, when the time remorselessly comes, of holding them in the palm of your hand for forty minutes?

But I want to say somewhere, and there might be worse places, that the gentle heart and the understanding spirit aren't as rare as you may gather from all this. There are happy times, when trains and planes and meeting cars are prompt, and hotels not only comfortable but expecting you. (Secretaries often book the room in their name, not yours, causing blank looks at Reception.) You are sometimes handed, with your key, a letter of welcome, offering help and comfort in all directions. Even flowers in the room. I had all this, I remember, in the Isle of Man, with a tour of the island thrown in, prettily guided, and a note when I got home which ended 'Come back soon'.

When it happens it makes up for everything, including clumps on the skull from check-in signboards, but the speaker has no entitlement to these civilities. It isn't because of this that he usually doesn't get them, but because the organisers assume him to be a tower of self-sufficiency, and the least of their problems. He's been told where, when, and how long, so now they can get on with the table decorations, raffle prizes, ironing the shrieks out of the public address system, and who is to join Mr Mayor in the group photograph.

Compulsive motorists, baffled by all this talk of railway trains, will have asked the obvious question, and dismissed me as a fool. Well, yes, I could drive, it's true.

Perhaps I haven't been fair to the train. It has its points . . . and provided they aren't frozen up, or there's a bout of non-cooperation by guards or drivers, the Inter-Cities are nearly all they're cracked up to be by the posters on, say, Retford Station. It's true that those metal-alloy buffet cars, an acoustician's joke, rattle the ear-drums like a xylophone hammer; that the staff is short, unhurried and resentful, and the carpet of paper plates and plastic spoons doesn't accord entirely with the refined inducements of BR's PR men. But for the public speaker, whether in his pre- or post-anxiety state, trains have two notable advantages over the motor car. You don't have to park them when you get to the other end, and with any luck – the absence, that chiefly means, of a couple of chatty fellow passengers with no papers to read but much to say on subjects close to their heart, such as purple sprouting broccoli, or the spread of illegal child-minding – you can go through your speech, and check your luggage as often as you like to see if it contains, or still contains, your evening trousers.

You can't do any of these things at the driving-wheel. 'My Lord Mayor, Gentlemen,' is as far as you get, because that's when the driver in front executes an unsignalled right turn, or the one behind suddenly overtakes, cuts in, brakes you to a halt, gets out, comes back, bangs on your window and says, 'I suppose you know you ran over a cat in Mitcham?'

I wouldn't give a painful example like that if it hadn't once happened to me on a wet night just outside the Oval. I was driving up to address a gathering in the humbler recesses of Caxton Hall. Mitcham was some way back by the time I got the news that I was a cat-killer – and then I never knew if it was true. The man who'd pursued me all that way to say so, or he gave that impression, seemed a little off-centre to me, in the pale wet lamplight. It occurred to me later that this was his regular technique for avenging

63

any supposed affront by fellow motorists. It was certainly a fine ploy, psychologically, because it upset me a good deal, and I was still brooding when I mounted the platform. Irrationally enough, I remember I was also trying to think whether I'd said I would speak for love or money.

It was a room of dark panels, I also recall, with a scattered audience that hardly signified turnaway business. There was an imposing lectern, of the kind more suited to the reading of major papers to the British Association, and on its shelf was a small envelope, not stuck down. Drawing forth what I took to be my speech notes, thinking in my preoccupied state that I'd already taken them, in their small envelope, from my pocket, I found a cheque for a pound. There was a certain restlessness in the shadows below during the pause that followed.

The period before a speech should be reflective. Two hours' drive in the rush hour along the North Circular Road isn't ideal for this, whether you kill any cats or not. I took that route early one Friday evening, to address some organisation for a friend of a friend. I forget now what they were. Traction engine rallyists, perhaps, or a local ginger group on street-furniture design. (Sociologists steamed up about what people are going to do with their leisure when the three-day week gets here can stop worrying.) I can't remember where this event took place, but I wouldn't rule out Foot's Cray, and if any of you saloon-bar map fiends, who can pass a whole evening's licensing hours discussing any given A to B, think I needn't have been on the North Circular to get to Foot's Cray from mid-Sussex, then you don't understand my navigation methods and we aren't talking the same language.

I know I arrived exhausted, entering the hall pale and scowling. I try not to do this, but it sometimes happens. The face of the friend's friend, alive with welcome, crumpled and fell. He rallied enough to say that it was good of me to come. 'I wouldn't come again,' I said, 'for a thousand pounds.' Though the words came from the heart they were only intended as a lead-in to a few comments on the North

64

Circular Road and all who drive on her: unfortunately he was called away without hearing the rest of it, and we never established any true rapport.

The friend, of course, who'd let me in for it, wasn't there. But another friend unexpectedly was. One long lost sight of, and not now on so much as a Christmas card basis: but he lived somewhere round there, had got wind of the occasion, and turned out to support me for old times' sake.

I've never had the courage to tell them, but this kind of thing is never as welcome as old friends may think. Strangers, you can fool and feel no pang: in good form, even play on as on an instrument. But it's no go, seeing the familiar face down there with its confidential smile. It means throwing out most of your best autobiographical stories, so many of which never happened to you and the face knows it. Churchill, it's said, watching an admired actor in Shakespeare, would sit in the front row following the text. Also, no doubt, with the best of intentions.

It was worse this time. He was a man who'd written a book, and sent me a copy, and I hoped I'd thanked him for it, because it had some pretty funny stuff in it: whose substance, and indeed more than one verbatim passage, I'd been passing off as my own for years, and had planned to do so again tonight. Impossible. It would have been as if Tom Jefferson, dropping in on a civics lecture in Philadelphia to support a friend, had heard him launch off with, 'We hold these truths to be self evident . . .'

So, all in all, it made for a thinnish performance. The sort you'd be glad, thinking it over in the crimson afterglow, that your friends had stayed away from.

It would be extravagant to blame the whole episode on the use of private transport, I realize that. The time when I had a back tyre explode in Solihull, several miles from a somewhat high-toned dinner there, and, on returning to the garage for my evening clothes and speech notes, found it locked for the night, is a better example of the dangers of driving to work. I can't think, now, why I should have chosen to drive there, when I could have trained from

Euston in an hour and a half, and all punctures mended free. An industrial dispute, perhaps. As it was, I remember taking two bites at it, pausing for the night at a hotel in Woodstock where even my American Express card came back to me looking surprised. And no more recoverable, that, than the £17.41 (I see from a quick glance at my accountant) handed next day to the Solihull Motor Company, Ltd. Reclaiming such sums is difficult for the speaker of sensibility: at all times, because his stock-in-trade – or mine, anyway – is an apparently natural jollity, a laughing disdain for life's little cheque-stubs: and this time more particularly, owing partly to the dressiness of the occasion, which I'd had to attend in a wrinkled brown suit, and for that reason failed on the whole to dominate. A man who makes a bad speech in a brown suit to a company in silks and satins, and in addition to his agreed fee asks for 380 miles at 8½p, hesitates to bring up the matter of night stops and blowouts.

The chief trouble with driving is distances. These are usually great. England's south-east corner may be high on the two-boat household and the private pool. But if it's culture you're after, in the sense of perpetuating the quaint custom of getting someone to stand up and talk to a lot of other people sitting down, well, you won't find a lot stirring south of a line Blackpool to Spurn Head.

I haven't yet spoken at Spurn Head. The local coast-guards' luncheon club may be dragging its feet a bit in getting started. But it's only a short row over the water from Grimsby, say, which rings daily with addresses on Taine, the American Novel, Twenty Years of Newscasting, and First Steps in Crocodile Stuffing, with slides. So they could come to some arrangement. Blackpool, owing to mismanagement all round, and a lack of attention to the local paper, I once addressed three times in the same month, and for a man who keeps meaning to write a new speech, but never gets far without finding it fading into all the surefire hunks of the old one, it was a matter of devout prayers against audience overlapping.

But who's going to drive to Blackpool, and get there in any fit state to utter more than the three words 'large pink gin'?

Engagements near at hand occur all too rarely. Sometimes it happens. Even in Sussex itself, or reasonably adjoining Surrey. But disposal of the weapon remains a problem. Only this summer I spent twenty minutes circling Tunbridge Wells town hall, where luncheon was imminent and my place card confidently waiting, while the speakers'

lady secretary, troubled but statuesque on the municipal steps, kept waving me in every time I drove round. I finally found a lodging in a dead end some streets off, and at home-going time, all ready for a happy return by pleasant, leafy by-ways, discovered my exit blocked by an unattended hedge-cutting vehicle.

I did once get a goodbye outside a building. Newcastle-upon-Tyne University, it was, where Tyne-Tees Television, as it then was, had asked me to sit in judgement on a debating competition. You get all sorts of work. The faculty were heavily represented, and came out to wave respectful farewells not so much to me as to the Lord Mayor, in whose Rolls I was being kindly given a lift back to the hotel. It wouldn't start. It was a great embarrassment for all. The faculty and his lordship kept up the waving for some time. I may have waved a bit, but not much. As the chauffeur unrolled his tool-kit and got under the car, I was more interested, or tried to be, in how long the professors would keep up the gestures of godspeed. They tailed off one by one, and went back into the building. His lordship and I talked of other matters, until the driver confessed defeat and hailed two cabs.

Even the shortest journeys mean parking the car. A twelve-mile drive to Hove, for the Young Liberals Wine and Cheese, sounds nothing. You can get there, given a fair crack of the whip, with nerves virtually unimpaired. But parking is just as much of a nightmare as it would be if you were in Glasgow for the Friends of the Victoria Infirmary. One answer at Hove is to put the thing into the local car-wash, but it justly advertises itself as the quickest in the world, and if you want to make it last through even a shortish speech you need to stretch things with a supplementary wax, polish, white-walling and carpet-beating, adding a pretty new penny, at that.

Strangely, a difficulty with parking in Brighton, another agreeably short-haul trip, is that there are too many car parks, as I found last year addressing some librarians, and haven't accepted anything down there since.

It went off well enough, and I left in moderate spirits, for me, buoyed by the prospect of being home in half an hour, on roads I knew like the back of my driving glove. Running lightly up the steep ramps to the car-park's seventh floor – running, because it was a frosty night, and personal transport fools you into leaving your swaddling clothes at home – and the seventh floor, because that's where the only vacancy always is – I congratulated myself on having made a mental plan of the car's position, particularly since the whole building seemed to be full of cars like mine, even before I'd added it.

Now it had gone. Or wasn't there. I hadn't registered that multi-storey car parks, all of identical design and painted yellow, cluster richly around Brighton's West Pier. It did occur to me, after a renewed search, and hopes raised by many packets of Men's Kleenex on back windowsills, and dashed again on realising that this is more or less standard equipment for blue Rovers, that there might be not one park but two. That there were actually four – and I needn't tell you which I found the car in, the ice glistening on my ear-lobes and my thigh muscles squealing like plucked mandrakes – was beyond my imagining. However, there are. Or were. Maybe eight by now, so look out, if you're down there for a whiff of ozone with a mere five or six hours in hand. Your next of kin could be turning out the air-sea rescue as you tramp those dim-lit concrete echoes.

I haven't been so frightened since the night I got lost after addressing some ladies of Minneapolis, none of whom was going my way home, that is, to the Northstar Hotel. As it was only five minutes' walk, I'd decided to walk it. It was late. No one else in that city of 450,000 souls had had the same idea. One or two had decided to run it, or near enough, with that fast stride affected by Americans caught out after the mugging curfew. When I said to any of them, 'Excuse me, but could you possibly – ?', they really ran.

Again, I'd taken the precaution, on the outward journey, of noting a landmark. At the end of 2nd Avenue South, where I had left the Northstar a mere calling distance behind me, was a street-wide municipal announcement saying STOP AT TRAFFIC LIGHTS. As the next thing was the traffic lights, which even American traffic stops at anyway, I remember that it struck me as a bit unnecessary. Not that I was complaining. It was a great board stuck in the air. As a guide back home it couldn't fail. Over-confidence, though. It was only after I'd returned under it, with the slight swagger of a man who knows his way about in an alien land, and found the hotel missing, that I looked up and saw that I was no longer in 2nd Avenue South, but was passing under another great board all the same. All the avenues had them, and the streets too, I shouldn't have been surprised. Soon, I too was running, my heels ringing on the empty, iron-cold pavements. It was another frosty night. When I leant, exhausted, on fire hydrants, they were white with rime.

I found the place in the end. You'll have guessed that. But once more that certain toll was taken. And I was off to Cincinnati in the morning. Where a strange thing happened, I might say. A girl in some distress stopped and asked me the way to West 6th Street. As I'd just left my hotel, which was in it, I was able to help. The bracing effect on my self-esteem did much to dim the horrors of the night before.

There is always, of course, the chauffeur-driven car. Well, not always. In fact not often, at least for me, though some speakers insist. You don't have to be marooned many times on Southport sands to see the sense of it. I haven't the confidence, myself, but if some well-heeled organisation, its garages packed with directors' deductible limousines, offers to peel me one off for the evening, I can be talked into it. Unwisely, as it often happens.

The television companies sometimes extend these intimations of grandeur, though whether or not producers say on the phone, 'Of course, we'll send a car', depends on the programme budget, your celebrity rating, shortness of notice, the tradition (now fading) of getting you there two hours before you're wanted, and the individual producer's power-mad glee at saying things like, 'Of course, we'll send a car'.

Early one November a BBC man said this to me on the phone, adding, 'Where shall I tell the driver to pick you up?' 'Well,' I said, 'I could get the 6.40 to Victoria and hang around the chemist's, near platform fifteen. Tell him I'll be wearing – '

He got impatient. 'No, no. I mean your house? Wiltshire, somewhere, is it?'

When we got this sorted out he said the car would be there at five, and hung up. The programme, a chat show I'd never seen and didn't say so, was to go out live at half-past ten, so it meant getting straight into the bath.

People sometimes can't find my house, I don't know why. I never have any trouble. So with strangers from London I generally hang around the front gate when arrival time gets near. This time it came and went, and the BBC car didn't do either until a quarter to six, but at least when it did I could look forward to slumping in the back seat and not fretting about navigation problems. This man would home in on Shepherd's Bush like a bird.

'Which way?' was the first thing he said. So I got out and got into the front seat. He seemed surprised to find we were bound for the Television Centre, being in fact nothing to do with the BBC except in a remotely affiliated sense. Sometimes they telephoned the taxi firm he worked for at East Grinstead, he said. And he gave me a fullish rundown on the character of the proprietor, I think a Mr Mower. He was chatty, this driver. It was, he said, one of the rewards of the job, meeting different people.

'How long have you been doing this?' I asked him. When they're chatty, I have to chat. I'd give anything to be a grunter, and let them run dry. He said he'd been doing it nearly a fortnight. Had he always been a driver? No, he said. We were making a U-turn at the time, to go back and read a signpost. School teacher, really, he said.

Once we hit Croydon he was lost almost continuously, and kept leaning over to wind my window down, so that I could ask small boys the way. It must have happened seven or eight times. They all gave the same answer. 'Penny for the guy.' (I said it was early November?) He got on the wrong side of the road after one of these stops. 'Been driving tourist coaches in Belgium,' he explained, and he was still expanding on that when we finally made Wood Lane.

At least my state of exhaustion after all this didn't matter much. Had it been the sort of discussion programme I'd been led to expect, two guests and a chairman in a half-hour inconclusion, with false laughter and a buttoned leatherette décor, I don't think I could have done it. As things turned out, it was one of those shows where pre-arranged audience participation is passed off (the producer imagines) as spontaneous interruption. Perversely, I didn't much care for this, either: I think I got twenty seconds in camera, and sought sympathy afterwards from a fellow guest, saying that I'd come all the way from Sussex for a wasted evening. He said he'd had less camera time than I had. And they'd flown him in from a conference in Oslo.

I was speaking in Bath the next day, so I slipped off quietly in case my driver sprang out on me for the return journey. I couldn't risk losing all that sleep while he yawed in and out of Berkshire and Bucks. A tube from White City, just across the road, seemed altogether a better idea.

I hoped the Oslo man hadn't worried too much about his appearance. He looked neat, as I recall, and easy on the lens, given the chance. I think I worry too much about TV, and it dates me, in an age when your modern performer makes no concessions, beyond re-knotting his neck-cloth and checking that his zip is at least pulled up part of the way. I'm easily thrown. If I catch sight of myself in the monitor with a naked collar-button, I'm so busy adjusting things and making a note to burn all my slippery ties that I miss the quizmaster asking me who painted this picture.

'Oh, sorry. Austin Reed?'

Even so, you can't guard against everything. Such as leaving two of your front teeth in a toasted bacon sandwich when you're due down Sunset Strip in four hours' time to 'guest', as Hollywood puts it, on a mammoth audience show.

When this happened I was lounging, at a publisher's expense, by the swimming pool of the Beverly Hills Hotel, pretending not to recognise Virginia Mayo and Ginger Rogers, adorning adjacent beach beds. I was just about to change tactics and throw them a flashing smile, when I looked down at the sandwich and saw trouble.

Back home, it wouldn't have mattered so much. For one thing, my dentist's a friend of mine, and would have stepped in and filled the gap. For another, I shouldn't have been expected, all too soon, to be baring my debonair British choppers on sixty-eight syndicated channels. I mention the

British bit, because the Englishman in America can't help feeling his position as an ambassador for the old country, and is often encouraged in this by the courteous reception he gets. I'd already been in one studio that day, when they played me on to the set with sixteen bars of 'Rule, Britannia'. Luckily this was pre-sandwich, because it isn't the sort of compliment you can acknowledge with a couple of your best teeth in your pocket. But whatever happened tonight, I should need a smile. And I hadn't long to get one, friendless in a strange city, six and a half thousand miles from home.

Still, I told myself, going into the hotel, this was a place where the importance of emergency dentistry must be recognised. My kind of trouble could be a matter of life and death for people like Tony Curtis or Paul Newman. The hotel, I imagined, would keep a team of white coats on standby, alert for instant crowning. They not only didn't, but had no suggestions. If I'd asked them for a Sherman tank they couldn't have been more at a loss, and I was in no position to use much personal charm on them in the circumstances. All they could say, for my comfort, was that it was a Saturday, when everything shut at half-past four anyway.

Then, who should I see sitting by the wood fire in the spacious vestibule – a nice Hollywood touch, those crackling logs; true, it was November, though seventy in the shade outside, with bees – but comedian Dick Van Dyke. He was waiting for someone. Anyone but me. I surprised him, I think, and he may still wonder about the English lunatic who accosted him out of the blue, yapping intimately of a dental crisis. He was sympathetic, and spoke highly of his own man, who had his surgery ten miles down the San Fernando valley and didn't work on Saturdays at all. He also gave me a very funny impersonation of a man doing a TV show with closed lips, and might have been even more helpful if the man he was waiting for hadn't then arrived.

So now it was the telephone, via the yellow pages, and it would only harrow you to hear of the time that took, as I drew blank after blank: and of the problems, in that hotel, of raising any coins for the slot. It was the last call that connected me with an angel in nurse's shape. Could I come right now, she said, and they could probably fix it. Could I? I was into a cab like soda from a siphon. So quick that I'd forgotten the dentist's name before the door slammed. But the address was the thing, and I'd got that. 435 North Roxbury, and drive like hell.

I might have guessed it wouldn't be as easy as that. 435 North Roxbury wasn't a nice little house set back from the road, with laurels, and a brass plate on the gate. It was a tower block. Only a pup, say ten storeys or so, but it was occupied entirely by dentists. It was a dentists' tower block. At a guess, it housed about two hundred. Only one of them was any good to me, and I'd forgotten his name.

Time was rushing by. On Stage 6 at KTLA-TV they'd already be setting up the cameras and fixing the lights. I went from floor to floor, reading doors, tapping on glass hatches and saying, 'Exchuse me, but are you exshpecting an Englishman?' By the time I'd found the right hatch the air of weekend run-down was marked. Girls were locking away trays of teeth and beginning to paint their fingernails.

It was done, though. I think I should say that now, and put you out of your misery. And the show didn't go off too badly, all things considered. Lynn Redgrave was on it, and I kept calling her Vanessa. Also Pierre Salinger, and I congratulated him on a book actually written' by Arthur Schlesinger, but there.

When they pushed me on, smiling my renovated smile, I knew I'd done right by my country. The jewel-encrusted hostess swept me with her glossy eyelashes and said, 'Well. If I'd asked Central Casting to send me an Englishman, they couldn't have done better.'

I didn't tell her how near she'd come to getting the kind with the stiff upper lip.

That Bath affair, just to get back into it for a moment, was some high-powered industrial convention, ending with a slap-up dinner, which was where I came in. Just. It was meeting-trouble again. My contact, representing the many well-heeled organisations involved, and writing under an embossed letter-heading that must have weighed an ounce a letter, had directed me to look for a uniformed driver at Bath station, wearing a Consolidated Cement (as it might be) cap badge.

I'd already been slightly unsettled at being thrown out of the train at Bath Spa, by an inspector who wouldn't let me stay in until we got to Bath itself. I was still checking my bag for things like black silk socks, and was prepared to be insistent. However, when he explained that Bath Spa *is* Bath itself, misleading though that may be, I scraped things together and alighted, with a pyjama leg trailing from the hastily closed suitcase. It could have been a useful mark of identification. I'll be carrying a bag with a pyjama leg hanging out.

Still, I didn't expect any difficulties this time. Several presumed dinner guests had come by the same train. They had no difficulty in identifying their limousines. They walked into them without even breaking step, their cases gliding as if by inanimate instinct into the driver's non-saluting hand. Soon there were only a couple of cars to go at. It's hard to read cap badges. It can mean close quarters to the point of nose-rubbing. One gets inflated ideas, of course. My idea had been that one driver would be meeting one arrival only, would hail me respectfully, and we should be away. Time passed. I tucked the pyjama leg back, at the same time checking for socks and not seeing any – you can't be thorough in those circumstances, but it was going to be a worry until I got there – while the two surviving chauffeurs stood around avoiding my eye.

In the end I had to make the approach. 'Consolidated Cement?' I said to one of them. He shook his head, whistling a snatch. The other one turned out at close range to be a bus inspector, who was only using the second car to lean on.

Eventually a man in a blue suit but no hat came round the station buildings unwrapping a small cylinder of peppermints, and asked me if I was Mr Bulstrode. I lied in the affirmative, and he got in the second car and drove us off.

'I was expecting someone from Consolidated Cement,' I said.

'That's right,' he said, taking his cap off the passenger seat and putting it on. It's even harder to read cap badges in a driving mirror, but the journey was just about long enough for me to sort out the reversed image. As far as I could make out, it said something like HARRAP.

Organisers of speaking occasions, I often think, don't worry enough about details of this kind.

Chapter 5

Professional Approaches

Lord Mancroft has said that a speech is like a love affair, easy enough to begin, but harder to bring to an end.

I've also said it, many times, and without telling the audience where I got it, unless dropping the peerage on them seemed a useful move at the time. And I only tell you so that I can say that I once told him, with an apology for pirating his material.

Not at all, he said gracefully. It wasn't his in the first place. He'd got it from one of those foot-of-page fillers in an international magazine. The first time he used it was at a superior banquet whose speeches were reported next morning, and he was just reading his when the magazine called up and said they'd like to use it as a foot-of-page filler. He agreed. I think he said they paid him twenty dollars.

I'm not sure that I go along with the sentiment. I agree it's hard to end a speech, and audiences the world over will have noticed this. Toast proposals are an exception. You can stop anywhere with those, ask the audience to be upstanding, and they'll be more than glad to. Responses, on the other hand, can stretch ahead endlessly, like an avenue of Watteau poplars, and not a sign of an arresting hay-stack to run into. The middle ground is the easiest, but it takes a long time to reach if your start's not right.

I both sympathise with and envy the serious speaker with a serious subject. Sympathise, because his only sign that the audience isn't sleeping is a little appreciative drumming on the tables when he mentions that the club is now in its fiftieth year, and looks forward with confidence to another fifty. Envy, because not going for laughs he can't be thrown by not getting them.

In my case, if I don't get a laugh in the first half-minute – or, if I've decided on that, a reaction of shock – I'm pretty well ready to take my life.

At the risk of never being able to use them again, let me give you a few openings from my files:

For an audience entirely feminine:

'I recently had the honour of addressing the inmates of Holloway gaol. So if any of you ladies have heard my talk before . . .'

For a debate at Cambridge on anything:

'It's a great honour and pleasure, Mr President, to be here in Oxford tonight. I'm sorry, I think that should be Leeds.'

(Endless variants, but judge your audience. See p. 115 for a bad mistake in the Cotswolds.)

For school parents' day:

'It's no joke, having to talk to a mixture of children and grown-ups. If you say anything complicated the grown-ups won't understand it.'

As a substitute speaker:

'What's the most depressing thing in the world? The bit of paper that drops out of your theatre programme and says that owing to the indisposition of Sir Laurence Olivier tonight's Othello will be played by someone you've never heard of.'

To churchmen:
'Some years ago, when I was a curate in Islington – I'm afraid a lot of this is going to be straight quotes from a book by the Archbishop of York – '

To birdlovers:
'The common porpoise, I was reading the other day, can't hear the upper notes of the piccolo. Naturally, I was very sorry to learn this, though it could be a useful way of starting a speech to porpoise-lovers. As things are, it's useless, and I shall begin this speech again.'

To birdlovers (after food and drink):
'I've been told that I needn't try to say anything orthinological. As it happens, I don't know anything ornolithigical, but that wasn't why you told me, was it, Madam Chairman? You just thought, at this stage of the proceedings, that I shouldn't be able to say a word like orlithigonical, and you see how wrong you were.'

Opening a new hotel:
'I think I can say that I'm the only gentleman here. I've got that inflexion wrong. The only gentleman here, I should have said, who's been in the Ladies Room. You can't eulogise a place like this unless you've been shown everything. It's very nice in there. We Gentlemen are going to have to wait outside longer than ever.'

For literary circles:
'A friend of Sidney and Beatrice Webb, calling unexpectedly, found them stark naked in the summer-house reading to each other from *Paradise Lost*. Is this getting too sexy? Would the gentlemen like to leave the room?'

For any cultural occasion:
'Sacha Guitry, the eminent French actor, poet, playwright, producer, novelist, film director and flâneur . . . I don't

know what flâneur means, but it puts the fear of God into audiences . . .'

All-purpose:

'I shall try not to be too long. If I am, just scribble a note and pass it up. (*Pause*) I'm sorry . . . I thought I saw one coming already.'

All-purpose:

'When I tell you that a Mr William Henry Waddington, who rowed in the university boat race of 1842, was later the French Ambassador to the Court of St James, you'll realise that anything can happen.'
    (This is true. And once its peculiar impact is made, you'll have to give the supporting evidence.)

Any toast:

'Mr President, Mr Founder-President, Mr Chairman, my Lords, my Lord Mayor, Distinguished Guests, Ladies and Gentlemen, if you will kindly charge your glasses we can get this thing over in no time.'

All-purpose, when speaking for money:

'I've come here tonight at considerable expense, but I understand you don't mind that . . .'

Enough. Send for complete list, and money back if not delighted. Cheeky stuff, a lot of it, and you'll understand why I've kept on about the need, in my case, for that mood of buoyant confidence so easily undermined.
    You were rocked a bit, I expect, by that last example. Well, it looks worse in print . . . and I haven't given you any of the grand material about the cost of living that it leads into so neatly. As a matter of fact, the thing can be put with even more effrontery. 'I realise, Ladies and Gentlemen, that there are three questions in your mind: Who's

this? Will he be worth hearing? And how much is he putting on the price of the ticket?'

I never tell them how much, which is cowardly, after the alarming promise of no holds barred. In the stunned pause during which they feared I was going to I have their full attention, like a tight-rope walker. They half hope I'll fall off, but there's a rustle of relief when I don't. Getting away with it is pleasing. Not just because of the balancing trick. It purges my secret shame at selling the spoken word. I don't really understand the shame. I sell the written word without a twinge – and the spoken, in any case, has to be written first. But there it is.

It's important not to push the gag too far.

I once did this when addressing the BBC Engineering Society, in the concert hall of Broadcasting House. I had been a little upset, I think, by the letter of invitation, which said that it didn't matter what I talked about: their last

speaker had been an explosives expert, with demonstrations. Fair enough. But there was a postscript, no doubt well-intentioned, assuring me that there was no risk of being broadcast. Well, I don't know about explosive experts, but my own feeling about talking in the concert hall of Broadcasting House is that I don't want the risk of *not* being broadcast, and preferably at the going rate.

Thus stung, if unreasonably, by that old lack of empathy between the speaker and the spoken to, I ran on somewhat with the money theme that night, finally getting into an area of mock indignation. How was I to know, I demanded, whether or not a silver collection would be taken up? Nothing had been said. (It had, actually, but that would have ruined the flow.) There were people, disgusting though it might seem, who stumped the country speaking for nothing. Nothing, that is, but arrant self-aggrandisement and the sound of their own voice. I hoped that I wasn't being insultingly taken for one of them.

The passage got away from me, frankly, and it kept building. It was going well with all who saw that it was a gag, but a few officers of the society gathered in an aisle for a strategic mutter, and one of them eventually hurried to the back of the hall and semaphored me with an envelope, mouthing the message, 'OK!'

I felt sorry about that. And displeased with myself. I should have taken more trouble with the fine tuning.

Once a year, in a hotel in Park Lane, strange rites are observed, some time between March and September, the close season for public speakers. Oh, we get shot down over a few charitable lawns in the summer, the vicarage garden fête, the Olde Englyshe Fayre, but even your committed money-grubber expects no reward there, other than an actionable photograph in the local paper as he pays out to lose at hoop-la.

But in Park Lane, at the lecture agency's party, events are openly geared to gain. The speakers parade in the ring, or ballroom, and club secretaries converge from afar to examine their eyes and teeth and make their autumn and winter selections. Very practical. And done with delicacy, of course. We aren't actually prodded, like Hereford bulls in the sale ring, but our lapel badges are there to be read, and though they proclaim no fee, each buyer has a price-list that does. Sensible enough. But you need special gifts to pass things off with a gay word, as those budget-minded

ladies take a glance at the badge, a tactful pace back to flip the catalogue, and a sharp indrawn breath before moving on to the next lot.

Well, it's a day out for them. And you've got to shop around these days. But I've only been once, and couldn't say whether I've gained or lost since then, by forcing them to buy me sight unseen.

Why speak for money? Broadly, it's either that or speak for nothing. I used to do a lot of this, and still do some. But one year's end I went through the files and found a hundred and twenty-six invitations. Not because I was particularly good at it. Sadly, that doesn't worry people as much as you'd think, especially if they run one of those societies – you'd be surprised how many – that swallow a speaker a fortnight. I hadn't said yes to half of them. But the letters saying no to the other half had taken their toll of time and energy.

Ask for money, somebody said, it would cut down the demand. So I did. And it did. Believe me. But I remember what a horrifying idea it seemed at the time, and a shudder or two stays with me still.

Why? People don't, so far as I know, expect interior decorators to drop in and do over the sitting room and dining recess for nothing, or invite the professional chef to run them up a little free supper for six on his night off. Writers are in any case much called on, like actors and musicians, to perform out of the kindness of their hearts. It's partly because the occupations of artists aren't generally regarded as work. Those who long to write, act or play concertos, think that being able to do it is its own reward. What a blissful life, seeing yourself in print, proclaiming 'O! for a Muse of fire', or throbbing out the Mendelssohn. Just having a good time, really. Why shouldn't the writer enjoy himself with a thousand words in a university rag magazine, a charity antiques sale catalogue, or take your pick of all those environmental pamphlets?

The trouble with living by words is that everyone uses them. Skills in other fields are self-evident. When we have our appendix removed, we know it's something we couldn't do, and we expect to get a bill from the man who can. But literacy being more or less general, the distinction isn't always made between words in any old order, as with racy letters from aunts, and words arranged for print.

And as to speeches, if your agency booking form says, as it often does, 'Duration, 1 hour', that's ten thousand words gone. Or half a short book. And with the printed page, remember, the reader does a lot of the work, lifting the words off the paper. With a speech, it's all you. The labourer is worthy of his hire.

Agencies do much valuable buffering, particularly in the blushful matter of brazening out the money ·side. Bless them for that. You could never do it. And yet, alas, when blushes are brightest, when it comes to actually pouching the loot, you're on your own. By the time they've done all the negotiations, sealed the bargain, and set in motion their sequence of coloured reminders, they can't cope with the accountancy. Getting the cheque is left to you. It's a difficult switch, on the day of the speech, from witty charmer to gimlet-eyed man of affairs. You can hear disc jockeys with the same problem, landed with a grim news flash in the middle of the happy anniversaries.

Are we sometimes a little cool with treasurers? Nothing personal. It's just that you can hang around Mesdames President and Chairman indefinitely, admiring their hair-dos and making a note for your wife (you tell them), about where they bought their delicious little silver shoes. But you can't do this with Madam Treasurer. It looks . . . well, you think it looks . . . as if you're sticking close to her handbag, with its lurking cheque already drawn and signed.

Sometimes it's only half signed, a fellow-signatory being needed. She must be somewhere, and if you'd like to come along . . . This means the humiliating progress from group to group of laughing members. Has anybody seen Mary? No. Why? Oh, I want her for Mr Er (waves cheque). Incidentally, says one of the husbands, I hear she's threatening to . . . (funny story about Mary and Jack, depending for its laugh on the obscure foibles of local society). And so to the next group, where the mention of Mary reminds someone of a suggestion for a different place-card policy next time, and do you realise that Joan forgot to put Enid's bottle of wine in the raffle, didn't you, Joan? Oh, she's gone. 'Joan, Joan!'

So you're in a dilemma here. Haunting the fringe of groups that may contain Mary is one thing. Tagging along to find Joan is another, and though it's important not to lose the treasurer you begin to feel an intruder.

Whether it's worse to have this sort of thing before or after the speech is hard to say. Before, you like to con-serve your social energies, which can be seriously drained by the prolonged affectation of ease and confidence among these carefree strangers. Before is also noisier. This is their night. It comes but once a year. Spirits are on the up-curve as party after party, fresh from the bath and a stiffening of home Martinis, come breezing in all eager for the treat: while you, with a day's journey behind you and a hard night to come, feel a dangerous dwindling of persona, and no wish to be presented around, at the high shout, as our distinguished speaker this evening who wants his money first.

Payment before the event has another embarrassment. As with bridegrooms, there is always an impulse to cut and run before things get final. Notionally, at least, escape is always open to the still unpaid. What's the worst that could happen if you slipped off now, into the cool, hushed night? Simply to be drummed out of the lecture agency, black-listed nationwide in the lobbies of the luncheon clubs. And the way things are this minute there's nothing you'd like better.

But once your palm is crossed, you're grappled with hoops of gold. This in itself can heighten the ordeal ahead. Your obligation now isn't just to get up and say something, but to say something worth money. As you're ready to believe, at the best of times, that nothing you say is worth saying, let alone paying, the glow in your pocket-book throbs like a wound. It isn't so bad, perhaps, if the deal is clinched really early in the evening. There are hearty treasurers who say, even on introduction, 'Ah, I've *got* something for *you*'. And though the blow is severe, dealt as it is among a cloud of witnesses, the bruise has time to fade.

Often the treasurer is shy. As shy as you are. She may have held office for years, Hon Treasurerships being the hardest buck to pass, but still can't bring herself to make the drop. You sympathise. You know she has the stuff, and won't be happy till you get it. You'd like to help, but you can't. These are proceedings that only she can initiate. Your part is to be on hand should the moment strike. Unobtrusively. And affecting an airy unconcern that can easily be overdone, thus stifling her half-impulse to get the thing over, and leaving you, at the end of the day, with nothing but her empty handshake.

This means you'll get it by post, the amount will be wrong, and difficult correspondence ensue. Your letter saying, in effect, thanks for the dough but it's ten quid short, needs to be composed with brain-racking care if it isn't to sour, in retrospect, even the jolliest of associations.

All the same, payment after the event is probably best, whether on the spot or through the mails. At least you're free of those fears, familiar during sagging passages of a pre-paid performance, that the committee will rise as one and demands its money back.

On the other hand, again, if you have to linger too long among the parting guests, your early radiance tarnished to a smear, they could think you were dissatisfied with the applause, and hope to squeeze a bit more from individual tributes. You'd prefer them to think you were waiting for the money, rather than that.

Is there a solution? Not really. Money is the hardest of life's hard facts. You can't mix it into social occasions. In fairness, it's sometimes done tastefully enough. I've turned out my bedtime pockets before now and found the cheque I thought I hadn't had, slipped in by sleight of hand when I wasn't looking.

But I've also had it passed down the length of the top table, to save a treasurer's blushes, and that's a tough one to handle. Thinking it's just a reminder to thank His Worship the Mayor for attending, you rip open the envelope and out springs the cheque, a shock for the Mayor's Good Lady, with whom you were at peak badinage, and who had no idea, until now, that you weren't up there in Northumberland just for a night out.

One answer is to avoid all direct dealing. Unfortunately, you only get the chance when your services are sought – and you'd love to know why, but can never ask – by some mammoth corporation, to give the winding-up speech at its staff college in leafy Warwickshire. As you might expect, with an organisation of such eminence and grandeur, it delegates the arrangements to public relations consultants.

'Dear Sir,' they write, in impeccable electric typewriting: 'I have been instructed to approach you by our esteemed client, International Extruded Barbiturates . . .'

They can sometimes run to three beautiful pages, these letters – and all wasted if you say no. Except that, I suppose, it's all charged out to IEB, whose chairman could cut costs no end by just lifting the telephone. Your own correspondence can't be charged out to anyone, and if you say yes, swayed perhaps by the writer's flowing tributes to his client, which often embody a short history of the company and the threat of a book about it if you don't watch out, you'll soon be getting through enough time and stationery to have written the speech.

Granted, you refer them to the agency, but whatever passes between them they only pass to you. So you then write to them both. And they both write back. And the PR people, in the nature of their profession, are always eager to involve you in meetings, after which, if you pass the presentability test, a fresh correspondence, but covering stale ground, is set up by their principals, who by this time are equally keen on meetings. It's understandable. This is to be, after all, a celebration of their silver jubilee as the world's largest producer of electric bagging machines. They're nervous about it. You're an unknown quantity. Naturally they don't want any jokes knocking the product, though of course your approach should be entirely light-hearted, and here are three copies of Lord Stuffham's last speech to the shareholders and it would be nice if you could refer to it. Well, it would. Looking it through, you can spot at least a dozen ripe chances to raise a laugh. But not of the sort they have in mind.

Strangely, despite the efficient air of the great business world in action, these jobs are always the ones you can't get the money for. As with diplomacy, the upper reaches of commerce have a certain leisureliness. Walk, don't run, to the conclusion of the exercise. Delegates will meet again on Tuesday week for further discussions on the crisis. Time and the hour run through the roughest day. In my father's house are many channels, and my cheque's stuck in one of them. If it were not so, I wouldn't be writing, two months after the event, asking the PR men to put a rocket up Amalgamated Residualised Twines and find out what's going on.

On the other hand, I had a bad moment during the run-up to a literary dinner in Harpenden, where an architect and his wife, in true kindliness, invited me to their home for a preliminary bracer. They were an agreeable pair. Laughter pealed amid the clink of glasses. Then another pair bowled briskly in, the husband carrying an open cheque book and asking, in the course of introductions, if I could lend him a pen.

Spoilt the atmosphere. Though, in practical terms, it had your captains of industry beaten all ends up.

Chapter 6

Into the Unknown

The sort of briefing those PR men are so anxious to impart, though it has its uses, isn't always what you want to know. Even the agency, helping you all it can with the availability of pianos, leaves loopholes for surprises. I once, in fact, gave a speech where I needed a piano to be available, to get off some sort of minor musical joke, though I now forget what. The piano was available all right, but on the floor of the hall, whereas I wanted it up on the platform, and began by appealing for a few strong-arm men to make the transfer. Unfortunately, whoever introduced me had over-painted my reputation for comedy. The audience only laughed. 'No, no,' I said. 'I mean it.' They fell about. It was pure Frankie Howerd, and I had to sing the illustrations in the end.

So a thorough interrogation of the organisers is always advisable before the event. You can often miss things, even so. I spoke in a purpose-built banqueting hall once where the only illumination, planned, no doubt, for an air of snugness, was from table lamps shaded in darkish amber. 'I hope,' said the Mayor – who was actually a Mayoress, but feminine designations are abandoned at this pitch of civic dignity – 'I hope you don't use notes. I always make a very short speech here, and memorise it.' Mine, according to instructions, was to run for thirty minutes. I had to pause pretty often, turning my back on the company, trying to catch a glimmer.

It hadn't occurred to me, until then, to ask beforehand if there'd be enough light to see by.

How far is one justified in putting questions on the shape of a room? Pretty far, though Hon Secretaries must groan at such quibblings. Is this man a lunatic? They have not, perhaps, as guests of honour, been suddenly confronted with the L-shaped room, where only a voice specially trained in turning corners will reach the ears in the short end.

Or there's the hell-shaped room, often long and thin. As you file into those*, Madam Chairman will often confide that they're trying a change tonight, by way of experiment. Whereas they usually ask their speakers – not that these are her words – to shout from one end, as into a tunnel, you're to be stationed tonight on the sidelines, in what you might call the net-cord-judge position, throwing a sentence to the right and a sentence to the left, ending up with Wim-

* Sometimes to a slow hand-clap, a tribal custom meant as an acclamation, but doing nothing for me.

bledon neck and an audience that's heard exactly half what you've been saying. They could be lucky, at that, but they've no way of knowing.

Still, there are always, or almost always, microphones. You naturally ask about them. But to use or not to use is something you often can't decide until the moment of utterance. There the thing is. You've been advised to use it, because the acoustics are bad. Also not to, because it kept sort of howling last time. The speaker before you, as she sits down, warm with relief, advises you to speak directly into it, and close, though you noticed that when she did so her every sibilant was a wolf whistle and her bangles rang like the cowbells of Tibet. A man you meet during the comfort interval, who fears, not groundlessly, that nobody has told you how much he himself is in demand as a speaker, confides that he never uses microphones, and always says that if a man can't bring an audience to heel off his own bat, he shouldn't be on his hind legs in the first place, ha-ha, what?

Make your own decision one way or the other, would be my advice. If only to avoid one of those amplified chats with the toastmaster, who swells to technological status these days just by trailing his cable around.

'PRAAAY SILENCE,' yells the redcoat, exulting in his natural lung-power . . . and more or less gets your name right. And then:

'You want the microphone, sir?'

'Well, I don't know. Do I?'

'Up to you, sir. It's here.'

'Is it switched on?'

'All switched on, sir. *(Much distorted)* Testing, testing. One, two, three, four.'

'Right. Thank you. Mr Chairman, ladies and – '

'Bit low for you, sir. Didn't realise how tall you was, sitting down. Let me just turn the – '

'It's all right. I'll do it.'

Terrific bang, as business end drops to the bottom of its retaining shaft. Followed by general laughter as speaker overdoes the correction and is seen waving the now detached portion like a football rattle.

'Let me have it, sir. It's a bit – '

'I can manage, thanks. *(Heavy breathing)* Nearly got it.'

'Mind the wine-glass, sir.'

Sound of a greenhouse being demolished.

'Sod the thing. Mr Chairman, ladies . . .'
It's a big success with the audience, and may be the only part of your speech referred to with approval at the end of the evening. This is no consolation. You've brought your own jokes. And if you've brought one about microphones, so much the better. Naturally, the most useful time to tell it is during all the messing about with the microphone, and if it isn't quite the success you'd hoped for, it's because you keep catching the on-off switch with your sleeve, and what they're receiving in the body of the hall loses a good deal:

'All this reminds   studio, with a very inexperienced
         out of water.   By the time we'd   Lord Attlee
         It wouldn't have mattered if   questionmaster's
foot just then   But at least it   by   inside the
top. So I always   never tasted rattlesnake' meat
either.'

Or you can always ignore it during these technical preliminaries, and shout a humorous remark well clear of it, and the longer the better. 'IT LOOKS AS IF WE HAVE A SLIGHT TECHNICAL HITCH HERE AT THE MOMENT, LADIES AND GENTLEMEN, BUT NORMAL SERVICE WILL BE RESTORED AS SOON AS POSSIBLE AND IN THE MEANTIME I MAY AS WELL PUT THE TIME-HONOURED QUESTION CAN YOU HEAR AT THE BACK, THOUGH I MUST SAY IT ALWAYS SEEMS A PRETTY SILLY QUESTION TO ME, BECAUSE IF YOU CAN'T HEAR AT THE BACK YOU CAN'T HEAR ME ASKING YOU IF YOU CAN HEAR AT THE BACK (laughter, possibly). IT'S SAID THAT A WELLS OF H. G. FRIEND, A FRIEND OF H. G. WELLS, BIDING HIS RICYCLE DOWN A STEEP HILL – '

Toastmaster: 'Testing, testing. One, two, three, four. I think you'll find we're OK now.'

He loves to get into the act, the toastmaster. It's natural enough. Put yourself in his place (not to say costume), with a voice like thunder and an exhaustive command of orders and decorations, and it must be agonising to stand around night after night hearing all those inferior performers, with only a few miserable seconds to show them up between speeches. It isn't so bad, perhaps, when he gets a real mouthful of honours and awards to loose off. You can do something with Her Majesty's Most Honourable Privy Councillor the Earl of Hastings and St Leonards, Knight Commander of the Royal Victorian Order, and the rest. 'Pray silence for Mr Jenks' cuts his participation to nothing.

This may explain why a member of that repressed brotherhood once said, as the applause died away, 'What a very, very lovely speech that was, ladies and gentlemen. I don't know when I've heard a better – and I hear 'undreds.' And then brought the microphone along for me.

Toastmasters promised in preliminary correspondence don't always materialise as fully fledged professionals. It's one of the many points worth checking. Your amateur toast-master is a force to be reckoned with. Usually a local wag and extrovert, he's an infallible scene-stealer, with his neat neighbourhood name-dropping and inscrutable allusions. Inscrutable, that is, to visiting speakers waiting to get up. He's only to say, 'And it wasn't even Easter', or, 'You'd have to ask Percy Foster's dog', and all eyes are streaming. As an outsider, you must buckle on your full armour of arrogance when you finally rise, if you aren't to feel that you're only being tolerated until the real hit of the evening comes round again.

My memory bank is full of bad experiences with microphones, but they have a sameness. I might mention one, chiefly because of its unique, for me, setting, which was

94

Bow Church, Cheapside. There, with honest reluctance, I agreed to deliver the oration at a memorial service for an old friend.

At least he'd have laughed, which no one else felt they could do in the circumstances.

One thing I ought to have found out beforehand is that the church of St Mary-le-Bow has two pulpits. I don't know why. One sermon at a time is enough for most of us.

As it happened I got there prudently early, with time in hand to case the joint. This was something I'd learnt after reading the lesson one Sunday at a United Nations Day service in Haywards Heath. The local representative of the then U Thant had told me the chapter and verse, and I'd had a home rehearsal or two in case of any nasty polysyllables, so when the moment came I was able to give them most of verse one from memory even as I reached the lectern:

'And I saw a new heaven and a new earth, for the first heaven and the first earth were passed away, and there was no more sea . . .'

Then I looked down, and there was no more lesson. Only a fool, no doubt, would have expected anybody to think of having the book open at the right place. Naturally nobody had. What I'd got there was Isaiah 55. 'Ho,'everyone that thirsteth.' It took some time to find the right bit. It's a long way from Isaiah 55 to Revelation 21.

Those two pulpits threw me. For a man who can dither ten minutes between a tie with spots and a tie with stripes, though I'd been spared that today, this was a major dilemma. I was standing in mid-aisle, feeling that I might be fixed there for good, held by the balance of equal magnetisms as in some elementary physics demonstration, when a verger glided from behind the scenes to align hassocks, and told me firmly that my address would be from the north pulpit.

Good. I only wanted someone to make my mind up, and

I spiralled up and down the stairs a few times, counting steps and judging risers, before arranging my notes on the tasselled cushion, noting the halter-microphone and testing if my head was small enough to pass through its loop. It wasn't. A lucky spot. I unclipped its clip, laid the instrument ready to hand, and was pewed conveniently near before the church filled with the friends of the deceased. Who were also mine, never a good thing.

Towards the end of the hymn that was to cue me, the Vicar loomed at my elbow and said, 'You'll be in that one.' It was the other one. There wasn't time to argue. Besides, seemliness is all, with this type of event. He explained later that the north pulpit, at that time on a sunny morning, could get powerfully heated up through a lens-like stained glass window. No doubt he knew best, and must have been an even greater man for detail than I am. It probably surprised him when I at once downed hymn books and headed for the north pulpit after all. I needed my notes.

Recovering them upset the timing a bit, and I was up there as the congregation sat, gazing up in solemn expectancy. So it was their turn to be surprised when I came down again to traverse the nave, wishing I'd thought not to wear heels with steel quarter-tips, and shortly surfaced in the other pulpit, which meant they all had to re-focus, crossing their legs the other way.

The south pulpit microphone wasn't only too small to take my head through its cord, but had a clip which had been pressed home strongly by an earlier preacher. I gave up at one point and tried to force it down round my neck, but it wouldn't pass the ears, and there was a wild moment or two when I was wearing it like a Jesus-freak headband. All this juggling would have mattered less if it hadn't been a permanently live mike. The church filled with mammoth snorts and scrapes, like a herd of truffling hogs, until with a burst of that abnormal strength said to visit madmen, I tore its couplings apart and wedged the thing in my waistcoat. It was something, I suppose, that this was a three-piece suit affair. (Why it, or any other ecclesiastical occasion, should have to be wired for sound is more mysterious than the Trinity. They say old Jack Wesley managed all right.) At the end, I detached the microphone with care and silently descended the steps. It did the same, though not silently. I'd got the cable in a double loop round my ankle.

What you need to top off a commemorative address is instant cover from the organ. Noble, sustained chords with trumpet stops. If there's ever a next time, I shall ask for these. As they weren't forthcoming, what topped this one off was the mike hitting every step. The amplified crashes must have been heard in the cellars of the Mansion House.

None of my friends ever referred to this. For some reason, that only seemed a way of drawing attention to it.

As a general rule, in the matter of knowing what's in store, it's wise to clear the mind of all preconceptions. In prospect, you can take things too lightly, for example, which may lead to another major blunder, the attempt to combine business with pleasure.

Invited to give away the prizes at my old school – unexpectedly, because when I left no one had suggested that they'd ever want me back – I slipped up on both counts.

First, though my recollection of speech days was dim, dating from the receipt of my only prize, Lockhart's *Life of Napoleon*, which I must read some time, I had the vague impression that they were small-scale affairs. Some old fink stood up in the Sixth Form classroom, said that the race wasn't always to the swift, and passed over a few cups and books to the resident swots. Old Moggy Moxon then gave the headmaster's summary of the term's achievements, which accorded with nothing we'd noticed at first-hand, and it was a matter of eating the last of our stale cake and making a token search for the other cricket boot before going home to forget the whole thing. But education has made great strides since those days. Though I didn't know it, I was letting myself in for something on the lines of a Royal Investiture, in a setting not unlike the Spanish Riding School.

Secondly, my wife came with me, feeling it would be a

good chance for a rare reunion with my sister, who lived nearby. Thirdly, we drove. And fourthly I thought I'd work out my speech on the way, and knock off a few note headings in the hotel that night. All this got well between me and the proper consideration of the event.

Speeches don't get written in cars, as I may have said. This one didn't get written at all until well into the morning of the speech day, and then only in the hard-won hush of the WC built into the outer wall of Lincoln Castle, three miles from the school, and twenty minutes from the speech.

How this came about is complicated, but to do with a conviction, on the girls' part, that the exercise was geared to a family reunion rather than a prize-giving.

My wife and I stayed at a hotel on the edge of Sherwood Forest, which I gladly deny any named publicity. The plan had been to settle in there, drive twenty miles to scoop up my sister and bring her back to dinner, take her home again in good time, and get down to the speech notes. One look at the dining room, which had crumbs instead of table cloths, showed that we must have our reunion dinner elsewhere. It took some arranging. Restaurants aren't thick on the ground in the Robin Hood country, though haunches of venison, eaten under trees after a prudent picking-over for arrow-heads, may still go well, for all I know. My sister, however, had heard of a remote roadhouse she'd always wanted to patronise. It proved to be a riot of juke-boxes, and to favour fixed-time eating sessions, as on cruise-ships. Next session, by the time we arrived, was at 9 p.m. An hour to kill.

Spared the tireless Stones and Beach Boys, I might have made good use of the delay, even if it meant retiring unsociably to a lonely table, with Scotch and scratch-pad. This was hardly on. We sat together and screamed at each other.

'What did you say? I can't hear.'
'I said the race wasn't always to the swift.'
'No, I mean about Marjorie's baby.'

All I remember about the meal was mountains of chips.

I calculated. If we got out by eleven, and did a sixty-mile round trip getting my sister home, we might make it back to the Maid Marion's Head by two in the morning. It was optimistic. Partly because the hotel was down one of seven roads splaying off a roundabout like the Japanese flag, and we naturally tried the wrong six first. Partly because it was locked and dark, and after much ringing of the non-ringing bell we had to find a door round the back and enter through a room full of bicycles. Was this place a staging post for a six-day cycle race? We were in no mood to speculate.

By torchlight we left a note at reception for a seven o'clock call, and at nine, after a poor start to the night's sleep, awoke of our own accord.

It was in this way that I came to be jotting down thoughts in the castle convenience, having sent the rest of the party, though time was short, to talk knitting-patterns in a handy café.

The school was in sight before my wife, loyally turning to the matter in hand, asked if I'd got my speech notes. She has these helpful moments. It took ten minutes to go back for them, and discover that they'd been stolen by finding. Off again, at law-breaking speed, I reflected bitterly on this ungentlemanly behaviour by Gents. Speech notes are useless to anyone but the speaker. At least for proper purposes. But there, as my sister said, if people pocket the glasses you leave in cabs, which can only mean conjunctivitis if they wear them . . . My wife said that one of the girls in her optician's . . .

One look at the car-park and I knew that this wasn't just a speech day, but a Grand Speech Day. Bishops were alighting from limousines. Here and there were chauffeurs. The Head and his senior staff stood expectantly under an awning. Expensive parents were entering the building with big, confident sons. We were introduced to a number of knights, later to flank me on the flower-decked platform.

At least I wasn't drunk. There had been talk, in correspondence, about sherry before the event, but it seemed to get lost somewhere. The sober condition, I have since thought, was the only distinction between my speech that day and the classic by Wodehouse's Gussie Fink-Nottle. And Gussie, you'll remember, decided to give one of the religious prize-winners a *viva* before handing him his reward. 'Let me test you, G. G. Simmons. Who was that What's-his-name, the chap who begat Thingummy?' But he was in a happier situation. He was smashed.

I've dismissed the impromptu speech as a myth. But make it shamelessly anecdotal and you can always say something. At least I didn't tell them the one about the man who came to make a speech and left his notes in the loo. What I did tell them I'm not sure, but the bishops dropped their eyes in their aprons once or twice, and the boys, after early surprise that a visiting old fink should know so much about the facts of life, proved one of my more appreciative audiences. My relations wished they'd worn bigger hats and sat nearer the back.

The presentations were again bedevilled by electronics. The equipment didn't fail. That might have been better. It was even kept alive during the handing over of the books, cups and geometry sets, which took a long, long time. I'd been told there'd be forty prize-winners. Or I may have misread the briefing. In the event, there were forty categories, each with generous sub-divisions. Hardly a boy, it seemed to me, failed to come clumping up for something, many of them repeatedly.

The short form of congratulation is soon exhausted. 'Well done, Parker', 'Good show, Reeves', 'Nice work, Tomlinson'. And when Tomlinson comes up for the third time you can't think of a thing. With the last dozen or two I didn't care what I said.

My party only asked me two questions on the journey back. Why did I keep trying to shake hands with the hand I was holding the prizes in? And what was the idea, with the last dozen or two, of saying, 'How are you', 'Good morning', and 'Thanks very much'?

Presentations, or, indeed, all operations involving something besides the actual speech, can mean surprises. Often the very something is a surprise, as with a sudden demand to judge the funniest-looking dog, when you were only geared to a five-minute sales talk for the RSPCA. And organisers don't know what trouble they can get you into. On one doggy occasion I had to rule on the animal looking most like its owner. 'Just a bit of harmless fun,' they said when I demurred. So I went ahead and murred, and lost the services of a reliable local plumber whose wife and dog I named the winners.

As with university debates, you can be trapped into award-giving occasions by the promise of celebrities. I wouldn't have gone, some years ago, for instance, to hand out the Crime Club's Silver Daggers at, I think, Grosvenor House, if the winning names hadn't included some of my most admired blood-and-thunderers. One of them, I know, was Eric Ambler, but I forget the rest. It's not important. They were all out of the country, as it happened, scripting in Hollywood, or studying Turkish local colour for their next body-in-the-Bosporous. They sent their agents instead, mostly pale, nervous women for whom my neatly tailored congratulations needed quick revision. It strikes a false note, telling a lady agent that you have no words to describe the delight she's given you over the years, literally true though that may be.

There was a gratifying sub-plot at the Crime Club dinner. I was a knight for a night, which must be the next best thing to being a king for a day. A lady detective-writer, bright and beautiful but shakily briefed, greeted me as my personal hostess, and led me at once to the bar. What would I have? Life in Fleet Street has long cured me of any diffidence about being a charge on the female billfold, so I told her. 'And a Campari-soda for Sir Basil,' she said to the barman.

I wouldn't have let it run, but introductions started. 'I don't believe you know Sir Basil?' Handshakes. Expressions of delight. 'Actually,' I began . . . Then there was some diversion, and it got away from me. A dilemma. Eager though I was to strike these false colours, it couldn't now be done without wounding the lady who'd run them up. Even the toastmaster flew them in the end. I think he must have been a beginner in the business, because he didn't ask my branch of the knightage or baronetcy. The short, plain handle was glory enough. So I was stuck with it, and reaped unwonted deference all round. Even iced water, that night, arrived at the double.

It was almost worth not meeting Ambler.

But you can't allow for everything, try as you may. The physical nature of the awards, for example.

After a fight with a demented lawnmower I took a pair of sprained wrists to a Peterborough engineering works, and spoke from a rostrum stacked with polished wooden boxes. They were tokens of company approval for star workers of the year. When I made to lift the first one I thought it had been glued down as a joke, but it was only full of machine-tools, estimated at half a hundredweight. Still, we grand old public speaking troupers have to brave things out. 'It gives me great pleasure,' I kept gritting, smiling in agony and keeping the feet together against rupture. The wrists held out until about the last couple of lifts, and I was proud of that. But you see what I mean. Use all the foresight going, and you can still forget to ask in advance how heavy the prizes are. Even Cicero probably missed that one.

Sometimes, if rarely, there's light relief. The distribution of TV Oscars, in a lowly form, once came my way: the annual awards, and I tell no lie, for top television commercials. It was a matter of passing out plaques. No trouble there, anyway in terms of manageability, though they weren't triumphs of design. Showbiz trophies, putting aside, perhaps, the Ascot Gold Cup, are best kept in cupboards.

This was at the Dorchester. Nothing but the best. Trumpets, a wealth of tinselling, and the winning movies thrown on to a cinema-size screen, as writers, producers, directors and cameramen marched up to collect their laurels. The light relief bit came when a cog slipped somewhere, and the loudspeaker announcements got out of phase with the screenings.

'And now, the creators of the fantastically successful "DOGGY CHUNKIES"!' Fanfare. Applause. Cries of *Vivat!* or the like. Half a dozen up-beat dinner-jackets rise from their table. On screen, in living colour, a soignée housewife pours brand-name ketchup over hubby's fishburger supper and is dragged passionately on to his lap as a consequence.

Throughout the long evening they didn't get one right. When the voice announced girdles or deodorants, the screen showed carpets and engine-oil. Fantastically successful ads for encyclopaedias in weekly parts turned out as chimps flogging tea-bags. Promised a little classic for the Milk Marketing Board, we got hairsprays.

Confusion built rapidly. Parties who sprang up beaming at the mention of cooking fats were halfway to the platform before it dawned that the picture was selling paint, and turned back to collide with the paint party who'd seen their picture but only now realised the credits weren't right. There were times when I had twelve claimants lined up, and was tempted to toss them a plaque to scramble for, like the bride's bouquet at an American wedding.

All in all, one of the better evenings.

Disgraceful, I see that, to take other people's disasters in this indulgent way. But they do the same with mine. Memories are short, and you'll have forgotten the power cuts of early 1972, not even have realised, perhaps, that they clashed in East Sussex with the opening of a local arts and crafts exhibition, and guess what local dupe was opening it.

Prospects seemed bright at first. According to decrees from the Central Electricity Generating Board, we should have power all right on the night, so I was able to affect cheerfulness when I rang the organiser with the usual questions, asking where, when, size of hall, number and sexes of audience, how many speeches, length of mine, dinner clothes or sweat shirts, microphone or raw larynx, any other business. I got no answers. The man was beside himself. The exhibition being somehow remotely under the aegis of the Ministry of Education, he'd had a sharp word from Whitehall saying that even if current was lurking in his wall plugs he wasn't to release it. 'All I can tell you,' he said, the voice urgently fading as he made to hang up, 'is that the whole thing will take place in the dark.'

There's something to be said for a new experience. Drawing an audience's attention to the delights of exhibits they couldn't see was certainly a challenge. I tore up the draft of my speech and did a new one, geared to the special difficulties of the occasion. It had good bits in it. 'Mr Chairman, ladies and gentlemen, extinguished guests . . .' And so to the fine civic spirit of people who could come here on a cold night to look at invisible folk-weaving when they could have been comfortable in their own homes with their feet in the gas oven . . . if not their heads, considering the state of the nationalised industries. Art, I proposed to declare, was the Light of the World (? story about going to see Holman Hunt's picture of the same name, and missing it because it was so unexpectedly small . . . size is not all, give me the miniature against the mural?) 'At this moment, Mr Chairman, the sun is shining brightly in Australia, but does it shine on anything more exquisite than the works we see here tonight, if only we could see them . . . ?'

Well, hasty stuff. But when it's a matter of making deadlines, the very making has its satisfactions, and I wasn't in bad heart, on the whole, until I arrived at the venue and saw electric light streaming brilliantly from all windows. Whitehall had relented. Use all the juice you need. It just hadn't occurred to anyone to pass on the good news to me. The speech was useless.

I use the word venue with reluctance, but I don't know what you'd have called that place otherwise. It was, as far as I could tell, two semi-detached dwelling houses turned into one, and dedicated as a temple of the arts at the ratepayers' expense. No sweeping changes had been made to the interior, and my remarks, such as they were, are the only ones I've delivered from an ordinary domestic staircase. I was supported by the organiser and the Chairman of the Council. It was a squeeze, all packed on one stair. Eventually I moved up one, for freedom of gesture, and the others stayed down. A trio of Olympic medallists. The art-going public stood with up-craned necks in what I took to have been the sitting room and small hall, the dining room and kitchen given over to paintings, pottery and embroidery, with metal work and marquetry in the usual offices.

At least my stairs were descending, which gave me an ascendancy, if I can put it like that. It wasn't as bad as having to shout waist-high from stairs coming up, though if the place had had a cellar, I wouldn't have been surprised at that.

Speakers before now, I'd like to bet, have been invited to dangle from helicopters.

Chapter 7

Out in Front

Audiences are funny.

I once saw Marie Löhr, as Calpurnia, fall through a chaise longue in an earnest modern play about Julius Caesar. It got a laugh that Victor Borge would have given his ears for. But even that was topped when Gielgud, playing Caesar in a grey flannel suit, moved elegantly to the up left entrance to receive the replacement chair, which was brought on behind him, down right, by a stage hand who had difficulty in catching his attention. The roof came in on that one, and they had to drop the curtain for a minute while the house recovered.

My heart, probably the only one, went out to a repertory actor in Mary Hayley Bell's *Duet for Two Hands*. He had a chilling scene, alone on the silent stage, affecting to hear supernatural music. Flesh was satisfactorily creeping when the rest of us heard it. Well, not it, exactly. The local Boys Brigade band, distant at first, perhaps a couple of streets off, struck up with bugles and drums. It drew near, was nigh, banged and blasted its way past the stage door, dwindled, and all too slowly died. The audience rolled in the aisles. Why not? They'd come for entertainment, and didn't mind how they got it.

Like actors, the speaker soon learns how generously the audience will rise to unrehearsed effects. His own may fail. They're always a gamble. But never the crockery crash from the kitchens, or a bout of loud sneezes by a man at the back.

One of Sheridan's characters in *The Critic* says, 'I open with a clock striking, to beget an awful attention in the audience.' It's not bad. The danger is that they'll all start comparing and winding watches. Even if not, all you need is a police siren passing the windows and they won't even notice the clock striking.

By an odd chance, just about the time when the Queen was once speaking in Calgary, putting in a good word for Canada's underprivileged Indians and having it obliterated by a low-flying jet, I was telling a luncheon of Adjustable Shelving executives the one about W. C. Fields and the Chinese laundry: or possibly Austen Chamberlain and the Grand Union Canal: it's not important. On the punch-line somebody knocked a bowl of geraniums off its decorative plinth.

Granted, the incidents aren't quite on a par and not only because of the status discrepancy. The Frank Whittle effect can blot you out for a full minute, and when it's over the audience has broken up into discussion groups on aircraft recognition. All the same, you'd be surprised how long it took even to get a shattered bowl of geraniums out of ear-shot, what with the management running hot-foot, the laughter, ironic cheers, people saying 'Are you all right?' (but not to me), helping to pick up the bits, and not facing my way again until the last speck of diversion had been moaned into the vacuum-cleaner.

I hadn't been going too badly up to then, though perhaps Fields and Chamberlain weren't the best people to chime in with adjustable shelving. No one will ever know. I abandoned them, and unlike Royal speeches mine don't get circulated in advance for the benefit of those who wonder what they missed when the plane went over, or the geraniums fell. But if I'd been Fields or Chamberlain in person, or Marshall Hall and F. E. Smith rolled into one, I couldn't have recaptured that audience in under ten minutes. Their attention was divided. They were half waiting for something else amusing. The Chairman might faint, or a dog get in.

Interruptions from British Rail are always well received, and it's a consideration, when engagements come up, to make sure they aren't at railway hotels. Even without that, you can get trains, as I found last autumn on a sultry evening in Colchester. I'd been mildly distracted for some time by the sight of three hundred ladies fanning themselves with the dinner menus, but it was only when I tugged my tie and came away with damp fingers that it seemed sensible to ask for windows to be opened.

I've been on the other end of window-opening before now, notably when standing in for a non-starter once at a local literary circle. I don't know what disaster had overtaken the man who was supposed to be there, but it had left things pretty late. It was after lunch on the day of the event that they came on the phone with the SOS.

It's one solution, in such emergencies, to say that you can't make a speech at four hours' notice (which astounds them: call yourself a speaker?). You offer instead to fill the gap by just answering questions. If they can't see the difference between ten thousand unaided words for solo voice and a series of short displays as the audience keeps lighting the blue paper and retiring immediately, well, you can't help that. It means, inevitably, being introduced as 'our one-man brains trust', but you've sat through worse preambles than that and sustained your death's-head grin. It also means making sure that some questions are asked, and you beg the organisers to look to it. They see the force of this, but usually want to know what kind of questions.

Unreasonably, no doubt, you feel that if they've thought of getting you, they ought to have a rough idea of what they're getting you for. All is vanity. For all they know, having had your name from another possible stand-in, who turned them down but threw you in as a sop, your speciality is the Life-Cycle of the Beaver, or Transport Through the Ages. In fact, though, the questions don't matter much.

They can usually be got round, and if you get the old chestnut about the difference between British and American humour, and you only come back with James Thurber's claim, when his eyesight was failing, that he'd once seen a cat rolling across Broadway in a striped tub, at least the Q and A form is preserved.

This time something went wrong. There weren't any Qs. Either the Chairman hadn't been able to think of any. Or he couldn't find volunteers to ask them. Or the volunteers had said they would, and then couldn't bring themselves. I don't know. When question-time after a speech yields no questions it isn't too bad. They've had their pound of flesh, and an alert chairman will quickly suggest that the dummies out front should, in that case, signify their appreciation in the usual way. This isn't good, because they've just signified it after the speech. But it's better than having made no speech at all, and the dummies still sitting there. Tonight they sat for a full minute. Novelists are always using that 'full minute'. Tick it off on your second-hand to see how long it takes.

'Oh, come now,' said the Chairman. And a woman at the back, yes, really at the back, rose up nobly at last. 'I was wondering,' she said, 'if we could have a window open?'

'Certainly, madam,' I said. And I hopped off the platform nimbly and personally ran to the back and opened one. Or tried to. They were tall, louvred windows worked with strings. You won't need to be told, in this advanced stage of our acquaintance, that I worked the wrong string, broke it, and sat down in a metal waste-paper bin.

It was one way of breaking the ice, and the questions came in quite well after that. There was one, I fancy, about the difference between British and American humour, which enabled me to tell them about W. C. Fields and the Chinese laundry. Or possibly Austen Chamberlain and the Grand Union Canal.

Nothing is wasted, as Alan Herbert used to say. Speaking to a Young Wives' Fellowship some time later, I told them, on what pretext I can't imagine, about the time I'd hopped from a platform to open a window and sat down in a waste-bin. Some wild impulse made me embark on a demonstration. But the literary circle's platform had been low. The Young Wives' was higher. And this was the occasion when the floor had been french-polished for dancing.

Just as it was mad to give that demonstration, so it was, at Colchester, to originate the idea of opening windows. For one thing, the windows thought most suitable, behind the top table, had heavy double-glazing to be lifted out, and though speakers should at all times strive for a superior detachment from the spoken to, it seemed wrong to stand idly by while Mesdames President and Hon Tombola Secretary struggled unaided, and I returned to the microphone damper than ever. The other thing was that a commendably frequent train service, connecting Liverpool Street with Ipswich and vice versa, now roared past the seat of my trousers, or so it seemed, whistling its two-tone Diesels. This was a wrecker. One gag falling under a train you can cover with an ad lib: 'Didn't Beeching ever get to work on this line?' (it needn't be good). After half a dozen, all you want is to catch the next train out of there.

When events of this kind conspire against you, their timing is a lesson to us all. I can't remember now the exactly judged point where the waiter pushed over the plinth, but I wouldn't be surprised to learn that I'd just said, 'Mr Fields was paying this laundry bill when he dropped his wallet . . .' Or, 'Mr Chamberlain thumped the dispatch-box . . .' (Crash! Dead on cue.) Sometimes it's the human voice, and this is a bitter thing, when it picks its moment perfectly – as you, a student of these skills, so often don't.

'I think the time has now come,' I once said to a concourse of diners, 'to bring these remarks to a close.' 'So long, then, Audrey,' cried a girl in a headscarf and white boots, leaving the kitchens for the staff exit – 'You've had me for tonight.' It was a big hit. Nobody could talk about anything else afterwards.

Drunks are difficult. Separate tables, increasingly a feature of public dining, encourage the gathering of like minds. At first the disturbance is hard to identify. Someone, you suspect, has brought in a transistor, not wishing to miss tonight's instalment of 'Study on 3'. But there are bouts of laughter where none was due. Singing can begin. All becomes clear during your pause after, 'But seriously, Mr Chairman,' when this gathers form as 'Lloyd George Knew My Father'. There's no way out of this one. Even an appealing glance at Mr Chairman isn't always wise. You can catch him on the point of joining in. Sit down, is all. You're only spoiling their evening.

I've only once had to rise above a fight, I'll say that. It was during the fateful evening at Pentonville, and at least a couple of friendly warders took my side and restored order. You can't rely on that kind of support at Service reunions. You're on your own.

Strictly, if you lose your audience to rival attractions, you've only yourself to blame. Let the trains, drunks, jets and geraniums do their worst. All you have to do is turn them to advantage with a witty impromptu. If you can. I can't, myself, though I often see afterwards how I could. Too late. Like so many good ideas.

Such as staying at home.

Would you think it important, or even necessary, to know the names of the club officials and other leading movers? I wouldn't, at one time. It's hardly a thing you can ask at the correspondence stage. Even on the day, it arouses misgivings in your host if you suddenly say to him, 'By the way, is there anybody here called Huntergarth?'

But you never learn all there is to be learnt about this business. I used to tell a minor story of a merely linking nature, papering over some tricky inconsequentiality, which needed a proper name to be attached to one of the characters. For some reason I hit on Huntergarth, and ran him for years without a breath of trouble. Then I trotted him out complacently at a dinner in Nelson, Lancs, and the whole place went up in hysterics.

The only thing worse than the laugh that doesn't come is the one that does when it shouldn't. What had I said?

Something accidentally filthy? I remembered, as a school-boy, hearing the curate's wife tell a parish audience that her husband, who had just spoken, was always rather obscene. Meaning obscure, it came out later. (Not that she got much of a laugh on that.) Or what had I done? Flung open my coat to reveal a dry-cleaner's tag hanging from my waistband? Something worse? I glanced down. Nothing. It was so simple that I wondered it had never caught me out before. A certain Huntergarth, it seemed, present that night to make things worse, was the society's great ripe character, famed in its annals for inexhaustible japes, jests and jocularities. For his fellow members, who knew themselves to be lumpish and claylike by comparison, the name was explosively evocative of the only Huntergarth they knew. It took a long time to get them back.

I've changed it to Nutbeam since then. It isn't right. It has an intrinsic comicality, which can misdirect the attention. And the story will never be the same for me without Huntergarth. But you can't be too careful. Once is enough, for the Nelson touch.

Audience size is a factor. I always ask about that. I think it must go back to a very early experience when I was living near Bournemouth, and didn't know enough to make inquiries of any kind. It might have been my first ever public speech, it's so long ago I can't remember. But I remember being flattered to be asked, so that dates it well back. It was some local organisation with an impressive title, as it might be the Southbourne and Christchurch Readers' Guild, or the Boscombe Circle for the Lively Arts. I know I took a lot of trouble over my material, and rehearsed at home a good deal, polishing the gestures, testing for range and resonance.

I was collected by what I took to be a hired car, and driven to a closed tobacconist's, and it wasn't until the driver unlocked the shop door and led me through into a back sitting room that I realised he was an officer of the organization. It was too late to apologise for having occupied the back seat. Anyway, three or four other people had followed hard on our heels. I sat, I remember, on the piano stool, as they talked among themselves. Soon joined by a sombre clergyman and his supposed thin son. He asked if I should be comfortable there. 'Fine,' I said. 'But shan't we be going in a minute?' All were baffled, and with every justification. I'd somehow got the idea that this was merely an assembly point, one of many, no doubt, in the organisation's catchment area, shortly to converge in their hundreds upon some great hall or theatre, with a swagged and beflowered platform. But the audience had already converged, in its full complement. This was it. I believe there were nine. They seemed to think it was a pretty good turn-out, and the tobacconist had quite a gaiety about him as he fetched an extra chair from the kitchen.

'All right, then, Mr Conway?' he said. But he was only asking the parson to introduce me with a prayer, which he did gracefully, giving thanks for the inestimable blessing of humour, and throwing in Ecclesiastes on a time to weep and a time to laugh, a time to mourn and a time to dance.

Then they all sat back and waited for the fun. I stood, anyway at first. That's how I'd seen myself. But it wasn't right. Too dominating. I didn't need the range and resonance. Gestures seemed out, apart from being cramped by a nearby standard lamp. So I sat too. The piano stool gave me an inch or two of elevation, but I've made a point of never speaking from one since.

In asking about numbers, it's wise to ask the size of the room as well. It might be a cinema, and an audience of a mere dozen. Not that organisers ever foretell small numbers. It could conflict with the terms of the invitation, which hinted that the whole community was beside itself at the prospect of your visit. Learn to interpret any evasions. If, instead of answering boldly, '400 approx', they dodge it with, 'An excellent turnout is anticipated', you're alerted for an opening gambit designed to draw the meagre faithful into the front rows. ('When two or three are gathered together, they might just as well gather in the best seats . . .'

'It's not that I think you want to see me, but I'd like to see you . . .' 'I quite understand your sitting within easy reach of the exit, but . . .')

Why do audiences always go for the rear of the hall? A throwback, perhaps, to old embarrassments, sacred and secular, when they've been ejected from those front pews in churches earmarked for the Squire and his relations, or seized on, in theatres, to join the magician on stage for the subtle removal of their braces.

I'm talking, for the moment, of the non-eating occasion. With luncheons and dinners you can be more confident. If the sale of tickets doesn't reach the Society's minimum subsistence level they'll probably cancel the whole thing, and let you know in good time. The day before, say.

Your only trouble there is another mysterious audience quirk – the reluctance, by those who have eaten with their backs to you, to turn their chairs round. This is a great underminer. Why won't they look at you? It's easy enough, if they wanted to. Not heavy, those chairs. Has someone been talking, who heard you once? You think of times when you yourself, down there below, couldn't raise your eyes to the speaker. But surely you *began* with an open mind before lapsing into cuticle-study?

'Perhaps you'd like to turn your chairs.'

It sounds easy, but could you say it? No. Once they did it, you'd see your blunder. Turned chairs mean heightened expectations, and you want to say, 'No, no, please don't bother, it's not going to be that good.' Should you say it? Go on, might get a laugh. Might not, though. Take you seriously, turn the chairs back again. Nightmare. It's just this kind of mental confusion that lands you with saying how delighted you are to be in Derby when you're actually in Ashton-under-Lyne.

And it's strange. You can get away with that trick on purpose, but not by accident, though even then it depends on your frivolous reputation having gone before you. If not, there can be trouble. I had some once in Gloucestershire. Said how delighted I was to be in . . . er . . . (theatrical glance at notes) . . . and my right-hand neighbour, looking daggers of civic pride, hissed up at me, 'Tewkesbury, Tewkesbury!'

But I was riding high that night, and brushed him aside to proceed as planned, welcoming members of the Caramel, Fudge and Edible Jellies Institute, only later corrected to the North Cotswolds Gliding Club. When you're on form, it's easy. You can tell them that your speech-writer's unfortunately been injured in a duel, which explains the error, or pretend to have been comparing scripts at a meeting of GADSKIS (Guild of After Dinner Speakers and Kindred Insufferable Show-Offs) and come away with somebody else's. When you're not, you could give them Edmund Burke at his finest, and might just as well be reading aloud from the Water Officers (Scotland) Compensation Act.

That evening at Tewkesbury, as it happened, a bright-looking girl at a nearby table had laughed early. It doesn't often happen, but there's nothing like it when it does. As the speech develops, you can set up quite a little conspiracy with a laughing girl, provided she's laughing when she's meant to. 'Here's another good bit coming up.' Convey that with a conniving glance, and off she goes, God bless her, one beat ahead of the rest.

You can sometimes get a shock afterwards, that's the only thing. She can lay a slim hand on your departing sleeve and turn out to be an ace reporter from the Cheltenham and Nailsworth Sentinel, who's only been leading you on for professional reasons, with a notebook under her napkin. Your past life, or about forty minutes of it, flashes before your eyes. You'd never have told that almost true story about the named Cabinet Minister and the Thames pleasure steamer if she hadn't been hanging on your lips like that. But can you now, after such a feast of *rapport*, go suddenly serious and ask her to forget it?

To find out if the press is going to be present is always advisable. The problem is to do it without suggesting that you want to be reported, when the truth is that you don't . . . unless, of course, for some particular reason you do. A book coming out, say. But you can bet you won't be, in that case. That's the time when your press-cutting carries a full account of the Mayor on his controversial street-lighting plan, and eight words at the end naming you as the speaker of the evening.

Sometimes the bright girl merely proves to be too bright, and asks you afterwards if you didn't get your facts wrong about the musical instruments of the Old Testament. So it's good that she's not from the *Sentinel*, but bad that she did her thesis last year on OT musical instruments. She would. Just your luck that you dragged in the sackbut tonight, and at a point, what's more, where you generally use a personal reminiscence of Sir Malcolm Sargent that even little Dr Smartypants couldn't have faulted.

Still. Learning all the time. Remember in future that the sackbut is struck, not blown: even if it does mean losing that small flight of fancy about Moses shaking the spit out of it.

But there can be crueller blows from those dollies. Having added cubits to your height with their delirious admiration, what they want to say when they come up for a private word is that they believe you used to know their Mummy. The decades reel back. Can they mean that girl, of about this age, with whom you once roamed the moonlit dunes at Skegness, to the distant strains of Butlin's band . . . ?

It's awful.

It can be worse, though. Old flames can turn up in person, and you should have known, by now, never to accept invitations that end, 'Trusting you will welcome this opportunity to return to the Haunts of your Youth, and to see some old familiar faces . . .'

They won't be that, of course. Not at first. You don't recognise her in the audience. If the statuesque matron in the pearl choker exhibits an over-intentness you assume she's a bit deaf, poor thing. It's only later, as she hovers with a secret smile between you and the Lord Lieutenant, that you begin to wonder. 'Remember me?' she says.

It takes time. Time has been the trouble. Strange how it's passed you by more or less untouched. Don't you still put 'Hair, blond' in your passport details? Whereas she, who once gave you – it comes back painfully, like a diver recovering from the bends – a blue leather horseshoe-shaped stud box . . .

You'd rather the Chairman had turned out to be a man you'd once borrowed a fiver from, and haven't run across since.

Index